First World War
and Army of Occupation
War Diary
France, Belgium and Germany

49 DIVISION
146 Infantry Brigade,
Brigade Machine Gun Company
27 January 1916 - 28 February 1918

WO95/2795/3

The Naval & Military Press Ltd
www.nmarchive.com
Published in association with The National Archives

Published by

The Naval & Military Press Ltd

Unit 10 Ridgewood Industrial Park,

Uckfield, East Sussex,

TN22 5QE England

Tel: +44 (0) 1825 749494

www.naval-military-press.com

www.nmarchive.com

This diary has been reprinted in facsimile from the original. Any imperfections are inevitably reproduced and the quality may fall short of modern type and cartographic standards.

© **Crown Copyright**
Images reproduced by permission of The National Archives, London, England, 2015.

Contents

Document type	Place/Title	Date From	Date To
Heading	WO95/2795/3 146th Brigade Machine Gun Company.		
Heading	49th Division 146th Infy Bde 146th Bde Mach. Gun Coy. Feb 1916-Feb 1918		
Heading	War Diary 146th Brigade Machine Gun Company. January 27-1916 to February 29-1916/Feb 1918		
War Diary		27/01/1916	29/02/1916
Heading	War Diary 146 Bde Machine Gun Company. March 1916		
War Diary		02/03/1916	29/03/1916
Heading	War Diary 146 Brigade Machine Gun Company. April 1916		
War Diary		01/04/1916	30/04/1916
Miscellaneous	D.A.G. 3rd Echelon.	01/06/1916	01/06/1916
War Diary	In the field	08/05/1916	18/05/1916
Heading	146th Brigade. 49th Division. 146th Brigade Machine Gun Company. June 1916		
War Diary	In the Field during on Month of June 1916	01/06/1916	30/06/1916
Heading	146th Inf. Bde. 49th Div. War Diary 146th Machine Gun Company. July 1916		
Miscellaneous	War Diaries and Records, D.A.G's Office.	01/08/1916	01/08/1916
War Diary		01/07/1916	02/07/1916
War Diary	Theipval Wood	02/07/1916	02/07/1916
War Diary	Aveluy Wood	03/07/1916	07/07/1916
War Diary	Martinsart Wood	07/07/1916	07/07/1916
War Diary	Authville	08/07/1916	22/07/1916
War Diary	Hedauville	23/07/1916	31/07/1916
Heading	146th Brigade 49th Division. 146th Brigade Machine Gun Company. August 1916		
Miscellaneous	Officer i/c War Diaries & Records G.H.Q.	04/09/1916	04/09/1916
War Diary	In the field	01/08/1916	03/08/1916
War Diary	Authille Sector	04/08/1916	19/08/1916
War Diary	Acheau	20/08/1916	26/08/1916
War Diary	Thiepval Sector	26/08/1916	31/08/1916
Heading	146th. Infantry Brigade 49th. Division 146th. Machine Gun Company September 1916		
Miscellaneous	War Diaries & Records. D.A.G. Base.	09/10/1916	09/10/1916
Heading	War Diary during the month of September 1916 of the 146th Machine Gun Company. Vol 9		
War Diary	Thiepval	01/09/1916	04/09/1916
War Diary	Forceville	05/09/1916	18/09/1916
War Diary	Hedauville	18/09/1916	20/09/1916
War Diary	Thiepval Wood.	21/09/1916	21/09/1916
War Diary	Coy. H.Q. Gordon Castle	22/09/1916	26/09/1916
War Diary	Thiepval Wood.	26/09/1916	28/09/1916
War Diary	Mailly Mailet Wood	29/09/1916	29/09/1916
War Diary	Arqueves	30/09/1916	30/09/1916
War Diary	Hamel	02/09/1916	04/09/1916
War Diary	Grenas	01/10/1916	01/10/1916
War Diary	Humbercourt	02/10/1916	05/10/1916
War Diary	Gaudiempre	06/10/1916	06/10/1916

War Diary	Fonquevillers	07/10/1916	11/10/1916
War Diary	Pd.	12/10/1916	12/10/1916
War Diary	Fonquevillers	13/10/1916	20/10/1916
War Diary	Bienvillers.	21/10/1916	31/10/1916
War Diary	Bienvillers-Au-Bois.	01/11/1916	30/11/1916
Heading	War Diary of 146th Machine Gun Company for December 1916. Vol 12		
War Diary	In the field	01/12/1916	31/12/1916
Heading	No. 146 Machine Gun Company. 49th Division. War Diary for December 1916		
Heading	War Diary of 146th Machine Gun Company For January 1917 Vol 13		
Miscellaneous	War Diary of - for - 1917		
War Diary	In the field	01/01/1917	31/01/1917
Heading	War Diary of 146th Machine Gun Company for February 1917. Vol 14		
War Diary	In the field	01/02/1917	21/02/1917
War Diary	Le Souich	22/02/1917	24/02/1917
War Diary	Bouquemaison	25/02/1917	25/02/1917
War Diary	Croissette	26/02/1917	26/02/1917
War Diary	Bailleul Lez-Pernes	27/02/1917	27/02/1917
War Diary	Paquet-Le-Grand.	28/02/1917	28/02/1917
Heading	War Diary of 146 Machine Gun Company for March 1917. Vol 15		
War Diary	Le Grand Pacaut.	01/03/1917	01/03/1917
War Diary	Laventie	02/03/1917	31/03/1917
Heading	War Diary of 146th Mach Gun Coy for April 1917. Vol 16		
War Diary	Laventie	01/04/1917	30/04/1917
War Diary	In the field	01/05/1917	31/05/1917
Miscellaneous	146th Machine Gun Company. Reference Operation Order No. 30 dated 3/5/17	03/05/1917	03/05/1917
Operation(al) Order(s)	146th Machine Gun Company. Operation Order No. 30. Ref Map Aubers 36.S.W.1. Left Sector.	03/05/1917	03/05/1917
Operation(al) Order(s)	146th Machine Gun Company. Operation Order No. 30. Ref. Map. Aubers 30.S.W.1		
Operation(al) Order(s)	146th Machine Gun Company. Operation Order No. 30. Ref Map Aubers 30.S.W.1	03/05/1917	03/05/1917
Operation(al) Order(s)	146th Machine Gun Company. Special Operation Order. No. 31	07/05/1917	07/05/1917
Miscellaneous	146th Machine Gun Company. Relief Table.	07/05/1917	07/05/1917
Operation(al) Order(s)	146th Machine Gun Company. Operation Order No. 32. Ref. Map Aubers 38.S.W.1	07/05/1917	07/05/1917
Heading	War Diary of 146th Machine Gun Coy for June 1917. Vol 18		
War Diary	Lelobes	01/06/1917	03/06/1917
War Diary	Laventie	04/06/1917	30/06/1917
Operation(al) Order(s)	146th Machine Gun Company. Operation Order No. 38	03/06/1917	03/06/1917
Miscellaneous			
Miscellaneous		11/06/1917	11/06/1917
Heading	War Diary of 146 Machine Gun Company for July 1917. Vol 19		
War Diary	Laventie	01/07/1917	10/07/1917
War Diary	Estaires	11/07/1917	12/07/1917
War Diary	Lestrem Loon Plage Mardick	13/07/1917	16/07/1917
War Diary	Leffrinkourcke	17/07/1917	17/07/1917

War Diary	Oost Dunkerke	18/07/1917	19/07/1917
War Diary	Niewport.	19/07/1917	31/07/1917
Operation(al) Order(s)	146th Machine Gun Company. Operation Order No. 47		
Heading	War Diary of 146 Mach Gun Coy for August 1917. Vol 20		
War Diary	Nieuport	01/08/1917	06/08/1917
War Diary	Leffrinckoucke	07/08/1917	14/08/1917
War Diary	Teteghem	15/08/1917	27/08/1917
War Diary	Ghyvelde	28/08/1917	31/08/1917
Heading	War Diary of 146 Machine Gun Coy for September 1917. Vol 21		
War Diary	Ghyvelde (Nord)	01/09/1917	30/09/1917
Heading	War Diary of 146 Machine Gun Coy for 1st to 31st October 1917. Vol 22		
Miscellaneous	146 Infantry Brigade.	31/10/1917	31/10/1917
War Diary	In the field	01/10/1917	31/10/1917
Heading	War Diary 146th Machine Gun Company. November 1917. Vol 23		
Miscellaneous	Headquarters 146th Infantry Brigade.	30/11/1917	30/11/1917
War Diary	Steenvoorde	01/11/1917	30/11/1917
Heading	War Diary of 146th Machine Gun Coy from Dec 1st to Dec 31st-17. Vol 24		
War Diary	Chateau Belge	01/12/1917	31/12/1917
Heading	146 M. Gun Coy. War Diary. Vol 25		
War Diary	Belgian	01/01/1918	01/01/1918
War Diary	Chateau. (Canal Area)	01/01/1918	14/01/1918
War Diary	Hazebrouck U.18.b.3.3	15/01/1918	31/01/1918
Heading	War Diary of 146 Mach Gun Coy for February 1918. Vol 26		
Heading	War Diary of 146th Machine Gun Company. From-1-2-18 To-28-2-18		
War Diary	Staple Area	01/02/1918	01/02/1918
War Diary	Moulle	01/02/1918	11/02/1918
War Diary	Staple Area	12/02/1918	22/02/1918
War Diary	Lonnebeke Sector	23/02/1918	28/02/1918

WO 95/2795/3
146th Brigade Machine Gun Company

49TH DIVISION
146TH INFY BDE

146TH BDE MACH. GUN COY.

FEB 1916-FEB 1918

49TH DIVISION
146TH INFY BDE

Confidential

War Diary.

146th Brigade Machine Gun Company.

January 27.1916. To February 29.1916.

Feb 1918

War Diary.
1/4 6. Bde. Machine Gun Company.

1916
Jany. Bn. G. Sections of 1/5, 1/6, 1/7 & 1/8 13"s West Yorkshire Regt detailed
27th. Officers + O.R. for transfer to M.G. Coy. Names of officers
O.C. Cap" MULLER. J. 1/8 13th W. yorks (Seconded as Bde M.G. Officer)
2/Lieut COOPER S.R. 1/7 " " " "
2/ " BELLERBY J.R. 1/8 " " " "
2/Lieut (Temp Lieut) GIBSON R.E. 1/7 " " " "
2/Lieut HILL M.W. 1/6 " " " "
2/Lieut ARMITAGE S. 1/5 " " " "
2/Lieut WARD D.E. 1/8 " " " "
2/Lieut (Temp Lieut) ANDERSON W.A 1/5 " " " "
2/Lieut THRESH A.E. 1/6 " " " "

Bde. Stationed at CALAIS under canvas.
Feb 1. Bde moved by train to AMIENS arriving 3. A.M.
2. Coy. marched to AILLY sur SOMME 2/Lieut COOPER struck off strength
9. Moved by march route to MOLLIENS au BOIS. sick.
10. do. BOUZINCOURT. Advance party to
12. Truches AUTHUILLE.
17. Took over Trenches from LEWIS Grps Sec" 17th NORTH" FUSILIERS.

1916 WAR DIARY. 14 6 Bde. M. Gun Coy. (2)
FEBY
13   14 8 Inf Bde. assumed command Trenches. 9 A.M.
14   Orders received that, except in case of attack, all machine gun
     fire to be done by Lewis Guns.
16   M.G. emplacements reported built & repaired.
to
29   No unusual occurrences to report.

J Mullen Capt.
O.C. 14 6 Bde. M.G. Coy.

2.3.16.

Confidential

War Diary.

146 Bde. Machine Gun Company.

MARCH 1916.

War Diary. 146 Bde. M.G. Coy.
March 1916

March.
2. Bombardment of M.G. emplacement at CATERPILLAR WOOD,
    AUTHUILLE. Emplacement pelisse out hit. No casualties.
    Capt Haigh No 2 Section showed great coolness during bombard-
    ment.

6. Company relieved by M.G. Coy 709 Inf. Bde as follows
    Reserve Section at MARTINSART } after relief Coy marched
    Trenches   } 3 Sections
    to HARPONVILLE + went into BILLETS for training.

16. Coy. moved by march Route to BEAUCOURT.
    Following officers seconded to 146 Bde M.G. Coy. (List 73) 28/1/16
      2/Lieut   Bellaby J.R.   1/8 Bn. W. Yorks Regt.
        "   (Temp Lieut) Groom R.C.   1/7   "   "   "
        "   HILL M.W.   1/6   "   "   "
        "   ARMITAGE S.   1/5   "   "   "
        "   WARD D.E.   1/8   "   "   "
        - (Temp Lieut) ANDERSON W.A   1/5   "   "   "
        "   THRESH A.E.   1/6   "   "   "

War Diary 146 Bde. M. Gun Company.
March 1916 Cont.
25. Company moved to BAVELINCOURT.
29 Company moved to Billets MOLLIENS au BOIS.

J. Mullen Capt.
O.C. 146 Bde. M.G. Coy.

2.4.16.

Confidential

War Diary.

No 6th Brigade Machine Gun Company.

APRIL 1916.

War Diary. 146th Bde. M. Gun Company.

APRIL 1916.

April
1. Company in Billets at MOLLIENS au BOIS.
6. Company moved to VIGNACOURT.
10. 2/Lieut BELLERBY assumed command during absence of O.C. on special leave
19. 2/Lieut BELLERBY handed over command on return of O.C.
20. 2/Lieut BONE F.T.F. Machine Gun Corps. taken on strength as a reinforcement officer.
21 }
to } Company continued training at VIGNACOURT.
30 }

J Mueller Capt.
O.C. 146 Bde M.G. Coy.

4.5.16.

D.A.G.
3rd Echelon.

War Diary of this Company for the month of May forwarded herewith

J. Mueller Cap¹ⁿ
O.C. 146th Bde M.G. Coy

146 BRIGADE
No. C9H
Date 1.6.16
MACHINE GUN COMPANY

Army Form C. 2118.

146 Bn M G Coy 44

WAR DIARY
or
INTELLIGENCE SUMMARY
(Erase heading not required.)

Vol 5

Place	Date	Hour	Summary of Events and Information	Remarks and references to Appendices
In the Field	May 1916	—	The Company remained in VIGNACOURT and carried out training in the neighbourhood during the month of May.	
	May 8th 1916	—	2/Lieut (Temp Lieut) R G Dobson 1/6 Battn West Yorks Regt was taken on the strength of the Company and assumed the duties of 2nd in command.	
	May 18th 1916	—	2/Lt H. L. S. Thomas Machine Gun Corps was taken on the strength of the Company.	

J Muller Capt
O.C. 146 Bde M.G. Coy

146th Brigade.
49th Division.

146th BRIGADE MACHINE GUN COMPANY

JUNE 1916

Army Form C.2118.

WAR DIARY
or
INTELLIGENCE SUMMARY

146 Bde M.G.Coy   June 1916.   Vol 6

Place	Date	Hour	Summary of Events and Information	Remarks and references to Appendices
			Training at Pignicourt. continued.	
			2nd Lieut Niels Dewhirst reported for duty on return from one month's leave on re-engagement.	
	Jun 19		Training at Pignicourt.	
	20		Training marched to PUCHEVILLERS. Billets reached at 2.30pm.	
	21		Training at PUCHEVILLERS.	
	22		2nd Lt (Temporary) R.G. Dobson seconded for duty as Second-in-Command from 1/6 West Yorks Regt. as from May 10th 1916.	
			Training continued.	
	23		Inspection of Company by G.O.C. 146th Inf Bde.	
			Billeted in PUCHEVILLERS (continued)	

146 BRIGADE MACHINE GUN COMPANY
No. ...
Date July 5 16

Army Form C. 2118.

WAR DIARY
or
INTELLIGENCE SUMMARY

(Erase heading not required.)

Instructions regarding War Diaries and Intelligence Summaries are contained in F. S. Regs., Part II. and the Staff Manual respectively. Title Pages will be prepared in manuscript.

Place	Date	Hour	Summary of Events and Information	Remarks and references to Appendices
	27		Moved at 10 P.M. to LEALVILLERS by march route.	
	28		Arrived LEALVILLERS at 2 A.M. Marched off at 9 A.M. for the Assembly Trenches in AVELUY WOOD. Bivouaced for the night.	
	29		Marched back to LEALVILLERS.	
	30		Marched to A group Trenches in AVELUY WOOD. Arrived 4-30 P.M.	

[Stamp: 146 BRIGADE MACHINE GUN COMPANY No. ... Date July 5 /16]

J. Muller Capt.
OC 146th Bde M G Coy

146th Inf.Bde.
49th Div.

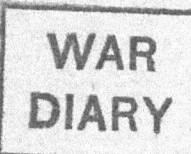

146th MACHINE GUN COMPANY.

J U L Y

1 9 1 6

49

6 M G Coy Army Form C. 2118.

Vol 7

To :—

War Diaries and Records,
D.A.G's Office.
G.H.Q. 3rd Echelon.

Herewith War Diary of this Unit for the

month of July 1916.

[signature]

O.C. 146th Machine Gun Company.

			Remarks and references to Appendices
On the field. 1/8/16.		6-30 a.m. A few ... ne.	
		...s in ELGIN AVENUE, THEIPVAL WOOD ...led, 3 wounded.	
	11-30 P.M.	When 2/GROOM arrived he found the Redoubt had been evacuated so returned. 2/WARD, D.E. and 2 guns ordered to A19 and B19 in German front and support lines to form a defensive line on exposed flank. The trenches had been evacuated and they walked into the enemy who fired, destroying 1 gun and wounding 2/WARD.	...ET. to R. ANCRE. ...by untiring work ...an interval of 1 hour
2ND	4-30 A.M.	2/GROOM reported his return.	

Ref. O.S.
Sheet. 57. D.
S.E.
1/20000.

Army Form C. 2118.

Instructions regarding War Diaries and Intelligence Summaries are contained in F. S. Regs., Part II. and the Staff Manual respectively. Title pages will be prepared in manuscript.

INTELLIGENCE SUMMARY.
(Erase heading not required.)

6 M G Coy   Vol 7   49

Place	Date	Hour	Summary of Events and Information	Remarks and references to Appendices
POSITION. ASSEMBLY TRENCHES AVELUY WOOD.	1916. JULY 1.		Prepared for action, and packed handcarts. Bombardment started 6-30a.m. A few enemy shrapnel in wood, and a few casualties in the Bde.	Ref. O.S. Sheet. 57.D S.E. 1/20000.
		7-30 A.M.	32nd. Division seen attacking South of Thiepval.	
		8-25.A.M.	Report received that 36th. Division had taken German second line.	
		9-0 A.M.	Moved from assembly trenches in AVELUY Wood to assembly trenches in ELGIN AVENUE. THIEPVAL WOOD crossing R. ANCRE by NORTH CAUSEWAY. Casualties:- O.R. 1killed, 3 wounded.	
		2-0 P.M.	8 guns sent to CHATEAU TRENCH. Heavily shelled.	
		2-30 P.M. do	2 guns sent to front line W. of THIEPVAL. 6 guns sent to second line trenches, CHATEAU TRENCH, ROSS STREET, to R.ANCRE. Lieut. DOBSON, and 2/Lieut. BELLERBY distinguished themselves by untiring work and coolness under heavy shell and gas shell fire.	
		9-30. P.M.	4 guns ordered to SCHWABEN REDOUBT. 2/Lieut. BELLERBY started with 2 guns and 2/GROOM followed at an interval of 1 hour When 2/GROOM arrived he found the Redoubt had been evacuated so returned.	
		11-30. P.M.	2/WARD, D.E. and 2 guns ordered to A19 and B19 in German front and support lines to form a defensive line on exposed flank. The trenches had been evacuated and they walked into the enemy who fired, destroying 1 gun and wounding 2/WARD.	
	2ND	4.30.A.M.	2/GROOM reported his return.	

Army Form C. 2118.

WAR DIARY
or
INTELLIGENCE SUMMARY.
(Erase heading not required.)

Instructions regarding War Diaries and Intelligence Summaries are contained in F. S. Regs., Part II. and the Staff Manual respectively. Title pages will be prepared in manuscript.

Place	Date	Hour	Summary of Events and Information	Remarks and references to Appendices
THEIPVAL WOOD	1916. 2ND			Map. Ref. O.S. 57.D. 1/20000 S.E.
		6.30 AM	L/Cpl. BEECH reported that his gun at ROSS CASTLE had been badly hit, but that he had got it and the team away. During the day the situation remained unchanged.	
		4-0 P.M.	O.C. 148th. Bde. M.G. Coy. taken round the 2nd. line trenches preparatory to relieving.	
		6-10 P.M.	2/Lieut. BELLERBY reported at Bde. H.Q. He stated that after going out to SCHWABEN REDOUBT his teams and some 30 Officers and Other Ranks of 1/5 West Yorks. Regt. under the C.O. were cut off and got separated from the rest of the Batt. in the dark and forced to retire. They moved down the German trenches in the direction of ST. PIERRE DIVION under continual shell fire, and were constantly subjected to bomb attacks. The guns were kept in action alternately during the retreat and held off all attacks. Finally owing to heavy casualties it was decided to quit the German trenches about A.20. ✳ (operation map.), and cross the open to PETERHEAD SAP. The party crossed man by man and all were got in except Pte. Gotch who was wounded and Pte. CREYKE who stayed behind as guard over the barricade they had put up. 2/Lieut BELLERBY WENT OUT two or three times to give water and bandage the wounded. He also took out a stretcher party after dusk and brought in Pte. GOTCH. 2/Lieut. BELLERBY recommended for D.S.O. No.2360 Pte. WALTON C. transferred to Coy. from 1/8th. Batt. West Yorks. Regt., and No.15844 Pte. GOTCH F.E. Machine Gun Corps. recommended for M.M. for gallentry during the retreat. At dusk No.1240 Pte. CREYKE R.✕ after dismantling one gun which was damaged brought in the other gun and a German prisoner. He finally carried his gun over two miles to rejoin the Company. Recommended for D.C.M.	✳ Q.24.6.22 ✕ attached from 1/6 TH Bn W.Y.R
		8-30 P.M.	Company was withdrawn and moved to bivouc in assembly trenches AVELUY WOOD, arriving at 10-30 p.m.	

Army Form C.2118.

WAR DIARY
or
INTELLIGENCE SUMMARY.
(Erase heading not required.)

Instructions regarding War Diaries and Intelligence Summaries are contained in F.S. Regs., Part II. and the Staff Manual respectively. Title pages will be prepared in manuscript.

Place	Date	Hour	Summary of Events and Information	Remarks and references to Appendices
AVELUY WOOD.	JULY 1916.			Map Refs O.S. 57.D. SE 1/20,000
		10-30AM	RE-inforcements of 20 officers and 15 Men were waiting here. L/Sgt. DIBB, D. No. 1242 (transferred to Coy. from 1/8th. Batt. West Yorks Regt.) recommended for D.C.M. for gallentry and coolness in assisting 2/GROOM to collect and bring in stragglers.	
	3RD	7-30AM	Coy. standing by to move up to line. Sgt. ROSS reported his team present but stated his gun in front line between THIEPVAL and R. ANCRE had been destroyed and the team burried. The Coy. stood by all day.	
		6.0.P.M.	Moved out to huts in WOOD behind MARTINSART.	
	4TH		Remained in huts MARTINSART. Lieut. DOBSON R.G. seconded from 1/6th.Batt. West Yorks. Regt. recommended for M.C. for gallantry and exellent work during the whole action although slightly wounded.	
	5TH		Remained in huts MARTINSART WOOD. 2/Lieut. THOMAS evacuated suffering effects of shrapnel wound received July 1st. Four guns were lost or Last gun received, bringing Coy. up to strength. destroyed during the action.	
	6TH		Huts AT MARTINSART WOOD.	
	7TH	8-30AM	Company ordered to stand by.	
		9-30AM	2 guns sent to each:- MC.MAHONS POST, MILL POST, NORTH, and SOUTH CAUSEWAY.	

T2134. Wt. W708—776. 500000. 4/15. Sir J. C. & S.

Army Form C. 2118.

WAR DIARY
or
INTELLIGENCE SUMMARY
(Erase heading not required.)

Instructions regarding War Diaries and Intelligence Summaries are contained in F.S. Regs., Part II. and the Staff Manual respectively. Title Pages will be prepared in manuscript.

Place	Date July 1916	Hour	Summary of Events and Information	Remarks and references to Appendices
MARTINSART WOOD	7TH	1-30.P.M.	Half Coy. recalled and reported in camp 5-30p.m. Very wet with thunder storms.	Map Ref. 57.D S.E. 1/20000
		10-0.P.M.	Coy. moved to trenches by POPLAR BRIDGE, TRAMWAY CORNER and thence to AUTHUILLE.	
AUTHUILLE	8TH	2-30.A.M.	Sent 12 guns to relieve No. 7. M.G. Coy. as follows:- ~~THIEPVAL and WOOD POST~~ 3 to WOOD POST, 6 to German line in LEIPZIG SALIENT and 3 to N near THIEPVAL AVENUE.	
do		5.0.P.M.	1 gun returned to Coy. H.Q. AUTHUILLE from LEIPZIG SALIENT. Heavy shelling during night. Practically no rifle fire or M.G. fire.	
	9TH		No4 Section relieved by No 2 Section in LEIPZIG SALIENT.	
	10TH		2 guns moved into front line at LEIPZIG SALIENT.	
	11TH		Nos. 1 and 3 Sections relieved by No. 4 and part of No. 1 section.	
	12TH	2-30.A.M.	Ordered to Stand To as the Salient was being attacked. Order Cancelled.	
do		3-30.A.M.	Sgt. Atkinson reported that KERERA St. had been blown up. Gun not damaged but tripod and spare parts box lost. Tripod recovered from No Mans Land	
		4-30.A.M.	N.W. of CRATER sent up to replace. Quiet day. 11-30p.m. Ordered to stand to as the SALIENT was being attacked.	
	13.	1-30.A.M.	Order to stand down received.	
		6.55.P.M.	Operation order for 1/7th.Bn.W.Y.R. to attack in SALIENT received.	
do	14TH	9-15.P.M.	3 M.Gs. moved out to reserve positions. 1 gun at Coy H.Q. in reserve. Attack by 1/7th.W.Y.R. commenced at 2-25.a.m. They bombed into enemy's lines but were driven back. No 4 Section put a barrage in R.31.C. at intervals to prevent any enemy crossing to our lines S. of LEIPZIG SALIENT. No.1 Section unable to fire ~~at~~ ~~5-10a.m.~~ on account of hostile shrapnel barrage.	
		9.30 -10.A.M.	Heavy rain. Front & reserve lines & AUTHUILLE very heavily shelled during ~~11~~ morning. Shelling at intervals during day.	
do	15TH	6.P.M.	Heavy firing to N.	
		3-30.A.M.	Heavy attack from N. down NO MANS LAND on the SALIENT. Sergt. HAIGH fired 1500 rounds, caught a good many enemy in the open & did good work His gun was bombed. Good co-operation with Stokes Mortar Battery. Message of congratulation on good work received from G.O.C. 146 Inf. Brigade.	

Army Form C. 2118.

WAR DIARY
or
INTELLIGENCE SUMMARY

(Erase heading not required.)

Instructions regarding War Diaries and Intelligence Summaries are contained in F. S. Regs., Part II. and the Staff Manual respectively. Title Pages will be prepared in manuscript.

Place	Date July	Hour	Summary of Events and Information	Remarks and references to Appendices
AUTHUILLE.	16TH	12-20.AM	Enemy again attacked but did not get into the open. Brigade line lengthened. 1 Section of the 148th M.G.Coy attached and all guns sent into line.	MAP Refs OS. 57.O. SE. 1/20,000
do	17TH	5-0.PM	All 4 guns of 148th M.G.Coy section reported in position. 2/Lt Groom suffering from slight shell shock, result of bombing attack. 4th Gloucesters took a piece of enemy front line trench on a front of 500 yards S. from X.7.b.9.9. Quiet day. Heavy shelling around Coy.H.Qs during night. 4th Gloucesters continued their advance, and took 250 prisoners. No 4 Section accounted for 27 Germans at 1300 yds from BOGGART-HOLE CLOUGH gun.	
	18TH	2-30.AM	Quiet day.	
		3-45PM	Received orders to move 2 guns from BURY St. to cover the NAB.	
do	19TH	9-0AM	Conference with G.O.C.146th Bde. as to method of attack and co-operation in small enterprise from SALIENT.	
	20TH	12-30.PM.	Orders for attack received. 2/Lt.Groom and 2 guns sent up to SALIENT at 6-45p.m. 2/Lt Bellerby from WOOD POST sector fired up towards MOUQUET FARM to cover working party of 1/6th W.Y.R. digging across valley to connect with advanced trenches taken by the 4th. Gloucesters.	
do		3-30AM	1/8th Bn W.Y.R. attacked under cover of T.M. and M.G.barrage and extended trenches held in LEIPZIG SALIENT. L/Sgt HAIGH slightly wounded while doing good work with barrage fire. Sgt Stembridge and L/Sgt Haigh both recommended for D.C.M.for gallantry during this action. Each of these guns put an enemy M.Gun out of action. Sgt STEMBRIDGE put up a barrage on enemy trench at 60 yds range and prevented our men from being bombed. Both guns caught small parties of the enemy climbing out of the trench into the open to escape the 1/8th.Bn. W.Y.R. bombers. These two guns and the other one sent up under L/Cpl BEECH between them fired 13000 rounds. During the day one emplacement was knocked in and three out of four guns in the WOOD POST sector heavily shelled.	
do	21ST	1-0PM	4th Gloucesters continued their attack. In the WOOD POST sector 2 guns fired during the night to assist the Gloucesters and to keep down their M.G.fire. One enemy M.G. was silenced. O.C. 148th M.G.Coy and Officers taken round the line.	

2449 Wt. W14957/Mg0 750,000 1/16 J.B.C. & A. Forms/C.2118/12.

…

WAR DIARY
or
INTELLIGENCE SUMMARY

(Erase heading not required.)

Army Form C. 2118.

Place	Date	Hour	Summary of Events and Information	Remarks and references to Appendices
AUTHUILLE	24th	11 a.m.	Relief by the 19th A.I.F.Company commenced, 3 section left in trenches at QUARRY POST sector. Relief complete without incident at 6-45 p.m.	
HEDAUVILLE	25th	10 a.m.	Company reported present in huts at HEDAUVILLE.	
	26th	10 a.m.	Rest billets. Ordered to stand to.	
			Still standing to.	
			Company (less one section) at Rest Camp at HEDAUVILLE.	
	28th		Ditto.	
	29th		Ditto.	
	30th		Ditto.	
	1st		Ditto.	
	2nd		Ditto.	
	3rd		Ditto.	

146th Brigade
49th Division

146th BRIGADE MACHINE GUN COMPANY

AUGUST 1 9 1 6

Officer i/c.
War Diaries & Records
GHQ

Herewith War Diary of this
Company for the month of
- August 1916

              R. Dobson Lieut
- In the field   for O.C. 146 M.G. Coy
  4/9/16

Army Form C. 2118.

WAR DIARY
or
INTELLIGENCE SUMMARY 146 M.G. Coy
(Erase heading not required.)

Instructions regarding War Diaries and Intelligence Summaries are contained in F.S. Regs., Part II. and the Staff Manual respectively. Title Pages will be prepared in manuscript.

Place	Date	Hour	Summary of Events and Information	Remarks and references to Appendices
In the Field	1/8/16	—	1. Company in Rest Camp at HEDAUVILLE.	
	2.		do. do.	
	3.		do. Received order to relieve 148th Machine Gun Company in AUTHUILLE Sector.	
AUTHUILLE Sector	4.	7-30 AM	Company (less one Section) marched to trenches to relieve 148th M.G. Coy. (less 1 Section)	
	5.	2 PM	Relief completed without incident. Took over 7 guns in LEIPZIG SALIENT. No. 2 Section reported having had several guns including one mounted near MOUQUET FARM. Two guns removed from Salient and placed in old British front line. Movement of guns completed 10-0 P.	
		10-30 P	One extra Section of the 148 M.G. Coy came under orders of 146 Coy and reported present in reserve at AUTHUILLE. Quiet night. Nothing of importance to record.	
	6.		Reconnaissance made to put in 2 guns of No. 4 Section M.M.G. Coy.	
	7.	11 PM	AUTHUILLE heavily shelled.	
	8.	4-0 AM 6-0 AM 4-30 AM	Heavy hostile shelling in reply to our smoke barrage. Arrangements made for Company and No. 7 Squadron M.M.Coy. to co-operate to assist in Australian Division the 12th Division's attack on trenches in direction of MOUQUET FARM. from SOUTH-EAST.	
		6-0 PM		

Army Form C. 2118.

WAR DIARY
or
INTELLIGENCE SUMMARY

(Erase heading not required.)

Instructions regarding War Diaries and Intelligence Summaries are contained in F. S. Regs., Part II. and the Staff Manual respectively. Title Pages will be prepared in manuscript.

No..................
Date..................

MACHINE GUN COMPANY

Place	Date	Hour	Summary of Events and Information	Remarks and references to Appendices
	8	9-23pm	Attack commenced — Machine Guns opened fire.	
	9	4 – AM	Heavy shelling by enemy. Quiet day.	
		12-30pm	2/Lieuts White and Jennings reported for duty.	
		11-59pm	Firing as on previous night to cover 4 Australians r The 12th Division.	
	10		a. Quiet day.	
		6-30pm to 7-30pm	2. AUTHUILLE heavily shelled.	
	11		Nothing of importance.	
	12		Quiet day.	
	13	9-30pm	Commenced firing to cover attack by the 12th Division and the 1/8 Battn W. YORK. R. — Two guns of 4th MG Battery also assisted Battn W. YORK. R. Two guns of 4th MG Battery also assisted in attack on LEFT BANK of R. ANCRE. Preliminary instructions for attack on LEFT BANK of R. ANCRE	
	14		Fired all night to assist attack by 48th Division on the right	
	15		Orders received for by 143. MG Coy & 148th MG Coy. O.C. 146 MG Coy inspected 6 night gun positions. Night firing as previous nights.	

WAR DIARY or INTELLIGENCE SUMMARY

Army Form C. 2118.

Place	Date	Hour	Summary of Events and Information	Remarks and references to Appendices
	16/8/16		6. Right guns relieved by 147.3 Coy. Relief by 148 Coy cancelled.	
		6.0 P.M.	No 4 Section took over positions at HAMEL from 147th Coy to fire on German wire on Left Bank of R. ANCRE. Quiet day.	
	17.		Quiet day.	
	18.	5. P.M.	Fired on communication trenches from THIEPVAL and the low ground near MOUQUET FARM. to assist very successful attack by 48th Div. Guns at HAMEL fired all night.	
		9. P.M.	Received orders for relief by 7th M.G. Coy. O.C. 7th Coy looked round the line.	
	19.	10 A.M.	Relief commenced. No 4 Section at HAMEL relieved by Section of the 7th Company. Company marched out to billets at ACHEUX WOOD.	
ACHEUX.	20.	9.0 A.M.	Carried out training at ACHEAU WOOD.	
	21.		do do do	
	22.		do do do	
	23.		Brigade practised attack on L. BANK of R. ANCRE. Trenches marked out at VARENNES.	
	24.		Divisional practice on ST. PIERRE DIVION.	
	25.		do do	
	26.	2.0 A.M.	Received orders to relieve 74 Coy in THIEPVAL Sector.	
		10.30 A.M.	Company marched out of Acheux Wood to the trenches. Relief commenced 5.30 p.m.	

Army Form C. 2118.

WAR DIARY
or
INTELLIGENCE SUMMARY
(Erase heading not required.)

Instructions regarding War Diaries and Intelligence Summaries are contained in F. S. Regs., Part II. and the Staff Manual respectively. Title Pages will be prepared in manuscript.

Place	Date	Hour	Summary of Events and Information	Remarks and references to Appendices
THIEPVAL Sector.	26.	6·P.M. 8·0.P.M	Communication and first line trenches heavily shelled and delayed relief. Relief completed.	
	27.	10 P.M. 10·45 P.M.	Gun of N°4 Section at HAMEL destroyed by shell fire Artillery very active on both sides.	
	28.	11·0 A.M. & 1·30 P.M.	THIEPVAL WOOD heavily shelled. Emplacement at top of CROMARTY AVENUE destroyed. N° 4 Section at HAMEL commenced making new emplacements. General activity by both sides. On trenches in front of THIEPVAL and up to South heavily shelled.	
	29.		Relieved by 147 th Coy. N°1 and 3 Sections into reserve at SOUTH WEST Corner of THIEPVAL WOOD. N°2 Section into positions on NORTH EDGE of WOOD. Coy H.Q moved into WOOD. N°4 Section continued to build emplacements at HAMEL. Meeting of CO's at Brigade H.Q°. Attack on LEFT BANK of R. ANCRE arranged for dawn on AUGUST 31st	
	30.	2·30 P.M	Meeting of C.O's at Brigade H.Q. Operation orders for attack on L. B of R. ANCRE issued and discussed. Message received preparing operations. Fired on german wire	

Army Form C. 2118.

WAR DIARY
or
INTELLIGENCE SUMMARY

(Erase heading not required.)

Place	Date	Hour	Summary of Events and Information	Remarks and references to Appendices
THIEPVAL SECTOR	31st		Wire cutting by artillery and mortars continued. General activity of artillery. 2 guns at HAMEL fired on wire. Eight guns of 6th MG Squadron. 4 on N edge of AVELUY WOOD and 4 near HAMEL [illegible] under 146 Bde to cover in operation	

for O C 146 Machine Gun Company

<u>146th. INFANTRY BRIGADE</u>

<u>49th. DIVISION</u>

<u>146th. MACHINE GUN COMPANY</u>

<u>S E P T E M B E R   1 9 1 6.</u>

War Diaries & Records.
D.A.G. Base.

Herewith WAR DIARY of this Company for the month

of SEPTEMBER 1916.

for Major.
Commanding 146th Machine Gun Company.

In the Field.
9/10/16.

Army Form C. 2118.

Vol 9

WAR DIARY
INTELLIGENCE SUMMARY
(Erase heading not required.)

Summary of Events and Information during the month of

SEPTEMBER. 1916.

of the

146th Machine Gun Company

WAR DIARY / INTELLIGENCE SUMMARY

Army Form C. 2118.

(Erase heading not required.) 146 Machine Gun Coy.

Summary of Events and Information for **September 1916**

Place	Date 1916	Hour	Summary of Events and Information	Remarks and references to Appendices
THIEPVAL	Sep 1		Meeting O.C.'s at Bde H.Q. to discuss plan of attack. Ground reconnoitred at HAMEL. Four guns fired all night on German wire in front of THIEPVAL WOOD.	Map 57. D.S.E
"	2		Arranged with 118 M.G. Coy for 4 S.A.A. gun teams to barrage German position in front of HAMEL after first stage of attack. Arrangements for attack completed.	See appendix
"	3	1.45 A.M.	Nos 1 & 3 Sections left Coy H.Q. (THIEPVAL WOOD) to take up positions in assembly Trenches. No 2 Section in Reserve. No 1 Sec on Left, No 3 Sec on Right. SPEYSIDE	
		5 A.M.	Reported to Bde all guns in position	
		5.10 A.M.	Barrage commenced. Sec No 1 & 3 maintain attack failed, escalade handed relief.	
		5.37	Two reserve guns moved into position between 16 A.W. Yorks The Reg. in British Old front line on Right.	
		5.45	Remaining 2 guns No 1 Sec moved into old British front line on left between 16 & 10 W. York Regt.	
		4.30 P.M.	Heard Battn (10th & 11th Lancs) reported German counter attack developing. The four remaining guns and four guns of No 2 Sec. were in position on parallel on Right Sector. No 1 Section also reported two guns in action on left sector	
		5.30	All guns in readiness to position in British front line.	
		"	No 2 Sec a withdrawn in Reserve into dugouts on left of front line. Two gun No 3 Sec. " " thin from 3p.m. No 1 Sec. 4 remaining in position last in anticipation of a further attack.	
		6.0	Attack cancelled orders received for relief by 165 Infantry Bde. Relief carried out on night Sep. 3/4. Total casualties 2 S.O.R. 2 guns destroyed by shell fire. 1 gun lost 2 guns ...	

Army Form C. 2118.

WAR DIARY
or
INTELLIGENCE SUMMARY

(Erase heading not required.) 146 Machine Gun Coy

Instructions regarding War Diaries and Intelligence Summaries are contained in F. S. Regs., Part II. and the Staff Manual respectively. Title Pages will be prepared in manuscript.

Place	Date 1916	Hour	Summary of Events and Information	Remarks and references to Appendices
THIEPVAL	Sept 4	A.M.	Arrangements made for relief by 148 B. M.G. Coy. No. 2 Sec" relieved No. 4 Sec" at HAMEL.	57 D. S.E.
		P.M. 9.0	Relief complete. Coy. less No. 2 Sec" moved to billets at FORCEVILLE.	
FORCEVILLE	5.		Coy. Training at Forceville.	
		P.M. 2.30	Lieut Hill (of No. 2 Sec".) & three O.R. wounded. Gun destroyed by shell fire.	
	6.		Training	
	7.		No. 2 Sec" relieved by No. 6 Squadron M.G. Corps.	
	8/10.		Training at Forceville	
	11.		2 guns No. 4 Sec" moved to Trenches between MESNIL & HAMEL to form a waiting S. of R. ANCRE under orders of 148 Bde. Training for Coy.	
	12.		2 guns No. 4 Sec" relieved (See " No. 4 MM G Batt") at HAMEL. Training Cont.	
	13		Training. Lieut Hill returned to duty from E.C.S. 2/Lieut J. R. OLIVER reported for duty, vice 2/Lieut J. R. Ballerby appointed 2nd in command 164 M.G. Coy.	
	14. 16. 17.		Training Cont. Sept 16. Capt MULLER returned to command after temporary absence from 11/8/16 attached Bde. Staff 146 Inf. Bde.	
	18.		Bde. moved to Billets HEDAUVILLE.	
HEDAUVILLE	19	A.M. 9.30	No. 3 Sec" left HEDAUVILLE to relieve Hog Sec" at ~~HAMMEL~~ 87 & 48 M.G. Coys on N. side of THIEPVAL WOOD. THIEPVAL Sector interested in anticipation of relieving the 14 B Bde.	

Army Form C. 2118.

WAR DIARY

INTELLIGENCE SUMMARY

(Erase heading not required.) 146. Machine Gun Coy.

Place	Date 1916	Hour	Summary of Events and Information	Remarks and references to Appendices
MEDAUVILLE	20		Major J. MULLER left the Coy to take up temporary duties J.M.G. Offr in II Corps. Lieut DOBSON unmounted Coy arrived in billets	57 D S.E
THIEPVAL WOOD. Coy H.Q. Gordon Castle	21.		Coy. relieved 14 B. M.G. Coy in THIEPVAL Sector with 1 Sub Sec at HAMEL (See 1. 14 B Coy attached for purpose of firing on German wire from HAMEL Considerable artillery activity on both sides.	
	22		Ditto	
	23	5 pm	Meeting J. at A.G. representatives from all M.G. Coys in 2nd Corps at AVELUY Chateau to arrange fire programme for attack on Thiepval.	
do	24.	7.45 AM 12.1 6.30	Orders received to relieve attached sec" of 148 M.G. Coy Thiepval Wood heavily shelled with gas shells.	
		8 AM	Attached section 148 M.G. Coy evacuated position to rejoin their Coy.	
		4 pm	Second meeting of M.G. Officers at AVELUY. Fire programme settled.	
do	25	5.0 PM 9.30 10.30 PM	Considerable artillery activity Orders for attack on Thiepval by 18th Div n received Final firm in front of Thiepval while tanks moved into position near Sent point Rd. No infl-- made.	
do	26.	5.45 AM 12.30 PM	G.O.C. at S.E. corner of Thiepval Wood dispersed working party near Crucifix Zero hour for attack on Thiepval. Sub Sec at HAMEL barraged ground N. of Thiepval Village	

WAR DIARY
INTELLIGENCE SUMMARY

(Erase heading not required.) 146 Machine Gun Coy.

Army Form C. 2118.

Place	Date	Hour	Summary of Events and Information	Remarks and references to Appendices
THIEPVAL WOOD	26 Cont.		4 guns on W. Edge of Thiepval Wood swept German trenches on Right bank of R. ANCRE. Right Sub Sec" near THIEPVAL AVENUE had several targets	Map 57.D.S.E.
		P.M. 12.45	during the attack. "CRÈME de MENTHE" ran over new emplacement. The other "Tank knocked" out main dug out.	
		1.30	About 10-0 prisoners surrendered to 2/Lieut C.P.SMITH (No. 4 Sec") who shewed them our tresols.	
	27	9.15	Guns in S.E. corner of Thiepval Wood inflicted numerous casualties on parties forming at N end of Thiepval villge. Germans put up Dummy Target here. Unusual artillery activity. No. M.G. Targets.	
			Moved 2 Right guns further to the Right as 18th D" n have crossed our front	
		5.0 P.M.	Received orders for relief by 74th M.G. Coy.	
		9.0 P.M.	Relief commenced. 74th Coy. had several casualties from shell fire during relief.	
do	28	A.M. 2.15	Relief complete. Coy. less 1 Off + 1 O.R. per gun moved into billets at MAILLY MAILLET WOOD.	
		P.M. 10.0	Rear party moved to billets.	
MAILLY MAILLET WOOD	29	9 A.M.	Entire advance turnover to ARQUEVES.	
		11 A.M.	Coy left MAILLY MAILLET WOOD arriving in ARQUEVES at 1.30 p.m.	
ARQUEVES	30		Coy. moved to GRENAS into billets	

Army Form C. 2118.

WAR DIARY
or
INTELLIGENCE SUMMARY

APPENDIX I

(Erase heading not required.) 1 + 6 Machine Gun Coy.

Instructions regarding War Diaries and Intelligence Summaries are contained in F. S. Regs., Part II. and the Staff Manual respectively. Title Pages will be prepared in manuscript.

Place	Date 1916	Hour	Summary of Events and Information	Remarks and references to Appendices
HAMEL	Sept. 2/3		Report of 2/Lieut SMITH commanding No 4 Sec.n which fired on the German lines # will S of R. ANCRE during the operations on Sep. 3. 1916	57 DSE
		A.M.	Fired normal night tasks on German wire S. of R. ANCRE as usual	
	3	5.10	German second line barrage for 5 minutes.	
		5.15	Fire lifted on to ST PIERRE DIVION & Communication Trenches leading to German Second Line.	
		9.30	Observation became possible as smoke lifted & during that attack had failed fire was re-opened on German Second Line.	
		P.M. 1.50	Germans seen moving towards their Front Line. Fire opened. From this hour onwards movement was very frequent & fire opened each time.	
	4.	8 A.M.	Germans observed moving in open from Second to Front Line. Fire opened. Germans returned to the trench.	

2449 Wt. W14957/M90 750,000 1/16 J.B.C. & A. Forms/C.2118/12.

Army Form C. 2118.

WAR DIARY
INTELLIGENCE SUMMARY
(Erase heading not required.) 146 Machine Gun Coy.

Vol 10

Place	Date	Hour	Summary of Events and Information	Remarks and references to Appendices
GRENAS	Oct 1		Coy moved to HUMBERCOURT	57D N.E
HUMBERCOURT	2		Cleaning up & Inspection in Billets.	
"	3		Major MULLER rejoined. 148 Bde. H.Q. at BIENVILLERS visited orders received for going into line. Orders received from 3 M.G. Coy. to be in line at one time each with 2 Sections in Reserve – 2 Sections up	
"	4		Billets. Preparing for move	
"	5	9.30 AM	Coy. less 2 Sections moved to Billets GAUDIEMPRÉ	
GAUDIEMPRÉ	6	10.AM	Nos 1 & 2 Section moved into line with Adv. Coy. H.Q at FONQUEVILLERS. Nos 3 & 4 Sections moved from HUMBERCOURT to GAUDIEMPRÉ arrived 11-30 A.M.	
FONQUEVILLERS	7		Indirect night firing on LA BRAYELLE FARM. Line very quiet.	
"	8		Indirect night firing on PIGEON WOOD, Road & Dump at E23d 6,2 & K4b 7,4 to K5a 2.8. DIVISIONAL guns reconnoitred for M.G. defence	
"	9		Night firing on GRANATEN HECKE E23d 2.4 – 5.8. Relief of 147 Bde. by 148 Inf Bde.	
"	10		Usual day & night firing Pigeon & Gommecourt Woods, Granaten Hecke, E 23, 24, 29 & 30 being quiet on in line.	
"	11		Fired on targets in E 23 d & Pigeon & Gommecourt Woods.	
" do	12		Fired on working Party E 23 c 7,5 & usual other targets (dumps & tracks).	

Army Form C. 2118.

WAR DIARY
INTELLIGENCE SUMMARY

(Erase heading not required.) 146 Machine Gun Coy.

Instructions regarding War Diaries and Intelligence Summaries are contained in F.S. Regs., Part II. and the Staff Manual respectively. Title Pages will be prepared in manuscript.

Place	Date	Hour	Summary of Events and Information	Remarks and references to Appendices
FONQUEVILLERS	13		Usual firing on E 23, 24, 28, 29, 30 & Squares K & 6. At Hostile Patrol E 23 c 2 9.	57. D.N.E
"	14.		Nos 3 & 4 Sections from Gonchiempre' relieved Nos 1 & 2. Seen in trenches. Usual Tasks + targets in E 23, 24, 28, 29 & 30 & K + 6.	
"	15.		Usual tasks + targets.	
"	16.		do.	
"	17.		do. E 23 c, E 29 a, E 30 at K & 6.	
"	18.		do. E 30 a 4 4, 26 c 55, 90, 30 & 60.88, 30 & 50, 68	
"	19.		All the Machine Gun Companies under orders and of 146 Infy Bde on relief of 147 Infy Bde. Wet all day. Arrangements made for readjustments of M. Gun Companies in the line. Half 148 Coy in reserve forced under control of 146 Bde. Two Sections 148 Coy from front line passed to control of 146 Bde on relief by 147 M. Gun Coy.	
"	20		146 Coy relieved two Sections 147 Coy in HANNESCAMPS Sector. One Section 147 Coy then relieved 146 M. Gun Coy in FONQUEVILLERS defenses. 146 M.G. Coy H.Q. and one Section moved into BIENVILLERS	
BIENVILLERS	21		G.O.C. 146 Infy Bde inspected most of the M.G. positions. Further arrangements made for second line defence of HANNESCAMPS.	

Army Form C. 2118.

WAR DIARY
or
INTELLIGENCE SUMMARY
(Erase heading not required.)

Instructions regarding War Diaries and Intelligence Summaries are contained in F. S. Regs., Part II. and the Staff Manual respectively. Title Pages will be prepared in manuscript.

Place	Date	Hour	Summary of Events and Information	Remarks and references to Appendices
			October 1916	
BIENVILLERS	22		Further rearrangements of Machine Guns made. Heavy gun fire all day.	57 DN.E
"	23		Arrangement proposed for concentration of M.G. fire on area about GOMMECOURT WOOD in conjunction with artillery barrage and smoke discharge to simulate bombardment preliminary to attack	
"	24	1.15 pm	Section reliefs complete. I red during the night on German wire, ESSARTS ROAD and village and on MONCHY AU BOIS. Major J MULLER proceeded to the Base	
"	25	2 pm	During morning fired on German aeroplane. Night firing on the "Z", ESSARTS village and communication trenches between ESSARTS and MONCHY	
"	26	2 pm - 3.36pm	Fired on GOMMECOURT WOOD in conjunction with Heavy Trench Mortars during night. Fired on the "Z" and ESSARTS	
"	27		One gun per seat detailed to antiaircraft firing during day. Night firing on ESSARTS and Comm. trenches. Very wet all day.	
"	28	1.30 pm	Section reliefs complete. Night firing on trench railways and trenches	

2449 Wt. W14957/M90 750,000 1/16 J.B.C. & A. Forms/C.2118/12.

Army Form C. 2118.

WAR DIARY
or
INTELLIGENCE SUMMARY

(Erase heading not required.)

Instructions regarding War Diaries and Intelligence Summaries are contained in F. S. Regs., Part II. and the Staff Manual respectively. Title Pages will be prepared in manuscript.

Place	Date	Hour	Summary of Events and Information	Remarks and references to Appendices
BENVILLERS	29	9.15 am	Working party in the "Z" dispersed with casualties.	57D N.E.
			Night firing on enemy tracks, ESSARTS village and LA BRAYELLE FARM	
	30	1 pm	ID. on having party near ADINFER WOOD dispersed	
		3.30 pm	Lieut. C.W.R. BALL (Machine Gun Corps) assumed command of No Company	
			Night firing on LA BRAYELLE FARM, PIGEON WOOD, roads and trench railways.	
	31		Very wet. Snow also falling in rapidly where not revetted.	
			Night firing on PIGEON WOOD, ESSARTS and tracks.	

2449 Wt. W14957/M90 750,000 1/16 J.B.C. & A. Forms/C.2118/12.

Army Form C. 2118.

146 M G Coy

XI

WAR DIARY
or
INTELLIGENCE SUMMARY

(Erase heading not required.)

Place	Date	Hour	Summary of Events and Information	Remarks and references to Appendices
BIENVILLERS-AU-BOIS.	Nov 1st		MAP REFERENCE. No. 57.D.N.E. SHEETS 1 & 2. (PARTS OF.) — NOVEMBER 1916. — Indes Section relief. Weather wet, trenches falling in. Night firing on communication trenches.	
	2.		Wet. Night firing on ESSARTS village and road, and the "Z".	
	3.		Firing on LA BRAYELLE FARM and light railways.	
	4.		New position for indirect firing by day. Commenced Position 150 yards behind front line near the HANNESCAMPS-MONCHY. Road. Night firing on communications as usual.	
	5.		Section Relief. Firing on LA BRAYELLE FARM. ESSARTS. Light railways and the OSIER BED.	
	6.	8-30 p.m.	Fired on enemy raiding party. One man killed. Night firing on ESSARTS ROAD and village, PIGEON WOOD, MONCHY-AU-BOIS, and the OSIER BED.	
	7	8-9 p.m.	3 Enemy machine guns silenced by our fire N. of FONQUEVILLERS. Weather still wet. Night firing on the "Z" and light railways and the OSIER BED.	
	8		Nothing unusual. Fired on enemy communications.	
	9.		Inter-Section relief.	

2449 Wt. W14957/M90 750,000 1/16 J.B.C. & A. Forms/C.2118/12.

Army Form C. 2118.

WAR DIARY
or
INTELLIGENCE SUMMARY

(Erase heading not required.)

Instructions regarding War Diaries and Intelligence Summaries are contained in F. S. Regs., Part II. and the Staff Manual respectively. Title Pages will be prepared in manuscript.

Place	Date	Hour	Summary of Events and Information	Remarks and references to Appendices
	10.		LIEUT DOBSON proceeded on leave. Firing on usual targets.	
	11.		LIEUT HILL returned from leave.	
	12.		Preparations for demonstration on GOMMECOURT further south.	
	13.		Demonstration on GOMMECOURT. 37,000 rounds expended. Inter-Section relief.	
	14.		Nothing unusual to report. Firing on communications.	
	15.		The rebuilding of an emplacement at E10.d.1.3. commenced.	
	16.		Firing on communications at night.	
	17.		Inter-Section relief.	
	18.		No unusual occurrence.	
	19.		"	
	20.		"	
	21.		"	
	22.		Inter Section Relief. Firing as usual.	
	23.	5 am	The enemy bombarded trench from LULU LANE to KENDAL with heavy trench mortars and guns of calibre 5.9" and 8". No damage to gun and no casualties.	
		6 am	Enemy raided.	

2449 Wt. W14957/M90 750,000 1/16 J.B.C. & A. Forms/C.2118/12.

Army Form C. 2118.

WAR DIARY
or
INTELLIGENCE SUMMARY
(Erase heading not required.)

Instructions regarding War Diaries and Intelligence Summaries are contained in F. S. Regs., Part II. and the Staff Manual respectively. Title Pages will be prepared in manuscript.

Place	Date	Hour	Summary of Events and Information	Remarks and references to Appendices
	23rd		C.M.G.O. was shown round part of the line. Lieut DOBSON returned from leave.	
	24.		2. Lewis gun teams with guns, reported for anti-aircraft duty. Firing by night on enemy communications. The G.O.C. 146 Infy Brigade, inspected the gun positions. Usual firing.	
	25.		Anti section relief. S.O.C. 146 Inf. Brigade inspected the gun positions. Usual firing.	
	26.		Lieut R. G. DOBSON proceeded to report to S.O.C. Machine Gun Training Centre, GRANTHAM. (Authority 49th Div. A/217/16.)	
	27.		Nothing usual to report.	
	28.		Preparations made for firing on communications in rear and on flanks of the following trenches to be bombarded on the 30 inst. VIS.	
	29.		E11.6 60.50 — E5.a. 55.05 E11.6 95.00 — E5.a 62.00.	
	30th		Lieuts. F.W. KING and J. R. JARVIE reported for duty. Position in ROBERTS AVENUE chosen. Operations to be carried out on 30th inst postponed. Nothing unusual.	

Charles W. Ryall L.
OC 146 Machine Gun Coy.

Vol 12

SECRET.

WAR DIARY.

OF

146th Machine Gun Company

FOR

December 1916.

Army Form C. 2118.

No. 146 MACHINE GUN COMPANY.

WAR DIARY
or
INTELLIGENCE SUMMARY

(Erase heading not required.)

Instructions regarding War Diaries and Intelligence Summaries are contained in F.S. Regs., Part II. and the Staff Manual respectively. Title Pages will be prepared in manuscript.

Place	Date	Hour	Summary of Events and Information	Remarks and references to Appendices
In the Field	December 1916			
	Dec 1st		Sharp frost and thick mist throughout the day. Demonstration by 49th Div: Artillery, Stokes Mortars, Machine Guns arranged for night Dec 1/2 postponed.	Ref Map 57 D. N.E
	Dec 2nd		Very cold. Nothing unusual occurred. Received orders for relief.	
	Dec 3rd		O.C. 138 M.G. Coy conducted round the lines before relief. Weather mild	
	Dec 4th		Operation Orders No 10 issued. BIENVILLERS heavily shelled between 12.30 and 2 pm. Weather mild	
	Dec 5th		Moved. Reliefs specified in No 10 Operation Order by 138 M.G. Coy took place. Teams relieved proceeded to PAS huts.	
	Dec 6th		Relief specified in No 10 Operation Order by 138 M.G. Coy took place. Relieved teams and Coy Head Quarters proceeded to PAS Huts.	
	Dec 7th		At 10 am Maps and 4 Sections proceeded from PAS HUTS and transport from GUADIEMPRÉ proceeded to BREVILLERS. Billets tumbledown + dirty	
	Dec 8th		Sorting stores and general cleaning up	
	Dec 9th		Company training from 28th NOVEMBER 1916. Very Wet day. Lieut M.W. Hill appointed 2 i/c with effect from	
	Dec 10th		Cleaning limbers for Inspection on 11th inst. C of E Service at 3.30 pm	
	Dec 11th		Inspection at 10 am by C.M.G.O. VII Corps. M.G. Stores overhauled. Very wet.	
	Dec 12th		Inspection of transport by O.C. 49th Div: Train. Section training	
	Dec 13th		No 1 Section on Range, remainder on Section training. Bright cold day	

2449 Wt. W14957/M90 750,000 1/16 J.B.C. & A. Forms/C.2118/12.

Army Form C. 2118.

WAR DIARY
or
INTELLIGENCE SUMMARY

(Erase heading not required.)

No. 146 MACHINE GUN COMPANY.

Place	Date	Hour	Summary of Events and Information	Remarks and references to Appendices
Lt. th. Guico	December 1916.			
	Dec 14th		No.2 Section on Range. Section training. Dull day.	
	Dec 15th		No.3 Section on Range. Section training. Very cold.	
	Dec 16th		Baths at LUCHEUX in morning. Football in afternoon.	
	Dec 17th		Kit inspection and inspection of rifles. Church parade afternoon.	
	Dec 18th		No.4 Section on Range. Section training.	
	Dec 19th		Section training. Very cold.	
	Dec 20th		No.1 Section on Range. Section training. Very cold.	
	Dec 21st		No.2 Section on Range. Section training. Weather milder	
	Dec 22nd		Section training. Very wet.	
	Dec 23rd		No.4 Section on Range. Section training.	
	Dec 24th		No.1 & 2 Sections on 400 yds Range. Remainder sections training	
			Divine Service 8.30 p.m.	
	Dec 25th		No parade. Company Christmas dinner and concert.	
	Dec 26th		Section training.	
	Dec 27th		Section training. Rangetaking & Special class on Range.	
	Dec 28th		Section training. No 3 & 4 Sections on 400 yds Range.	
			12 midnight orders received to move to GROUCHES. Command by Lieut M.W. 14166 Capt C.W.R. BALL. during the absence on leave of	

2449 Wt. W14957/M90 750,000 1/16 J.B.C. & R. Forms/C.2118/12.

Army Form C. 2118.

No. 146 MACHINE GUN COMPANY.

WAR DIARY
or
INTELLIGENCE SUMMARY

(Erase heading not required.)

Instructions regarding War Diaries and Intelligence Summaries are contained in F. S. Regs., Part II. and the Staff Manual respectively. Title Pages will be prepared in manuscript.

Place	Date	Hour	Summary of Events and Information	Remarks and references to Appendices
	Jan. 29th		Company moved to GROUCHES. Owing to insufficient accommodation permission was asked for to move to BOUT DE PRES.	
	Jan. 30th		Company moved to BOUT DE PRES.	
	Jan. 31st		Sunday. Company settling into billets. German gun and mounting received on loan from C.M.G.O. VII Corps. for instructional purposes.	

Moxhie
Lieut.
O.C. 146th Machine Gun Company.
31/1/2/16.

No. 146
MACHINE GUN
COMPANY.

49th Division

original

War Diary
for December 1916.

Vol 13

SECRET.

WAR DIARY.

OF

146th Machine Gun Company

FOR

January 1917.

SECRET.

WAR DIARY.

OF

FOR

1917.

WAR DIARY
or
INTELLIGENCE SUMMARY

Army Form C. 2118.

146th Machine Gun Company

Place	Date 1917	Hour	Summary of Events and Information	Remarks and references to Appendices
In the Field	Jan 1st		Company training at BOUT DE PRES. Transport taken over by Brigade Commander.	LENS 1/40000
	2nd		Company training. Company actively attached action from Lindens carried out. Lectures given to Officers & NCOs On or Carnage Musketry gun set up by C.M.G.O. VII Corps.	BAMIRVILLE 1/10000
	3rd		Section training. Orders received to proceed to BAILLEULMONT to view the line to be taken over on 4th inst.	
	4th		O.C. & two section Officers visited BAILLEULMONT and positions of Sgt No 4 Coy on the line.	
	5th		Company training and preparations for move.	
	6th		Nos 1 & 3 Sections moved to BAILLEULMONT preparatory to relief of Sections 2 of Machine Gun Company.	
	7th		Nos 1 & 3 Sections relieved Sections 2 of Machine gun Company 2, position being taken over by the two sections.	
	8th		H.Q. & No 2 & 4 sections moved to BAILLEULMONT.	
	9th		11.30 am Relief of the 2nd Machine Gun Company by the Company completed.	

Murdoch [?]
for O.C. 146th Machine Gun Coy.

Army Form C. 2118.

WAR DIARY
or
INTELLIGENCE SUMMARY 146th Machine Gun Company

(Erase heading not required.)

Place	Date	Hour	Summary of Events and Information	Remarks and references to Appendices
In the Forest			All positions reached by OC Company and report made to 146th Infantry Brigade as to advisability of method of holding up an attack by machine gun barrage fire before positions received to "Bank Out" the barrage method also to carry on with normal device for method.	
		10ᵃ	Orders received to meet C.M.G.O. VII Corps at Brigade Headquarters to arrange for carrying out of combined Artillery + M.G. fire on German positions at X.Z.C. (BLAIRVILLE ½000) Details arranged and arrangements made to carry out ranging fire on following day with observation from positions taken over from 148 M.G. Coy having J12 in all. Ranging has impossible owing to low visibility.	
		11ᵃ 15ᵃ	Firing of German line — front and support and dumps the day and on roads by night carried out — seven guns in all being in action. Total of 8 rounds fired 14,500. Command of Company received by Capt. E.W.R. Ball or others from local.	
		15ᵃ	Nothing of importance happened. Work was carried on at intervals. Reconn. carried out in cooperation with OC Suisanes Company to assure that cooperation of the machine gun with infantry of Brigade in the event of the capture of the line by the third Brigade was complete.	

Mitchell Lieut
A.T. 146 Machine Gun Coy

Army Form C. 2118.

WAR DIARY
or
INTELLIGENCE SUMMARY
(Erase heading not required.)

146th Machine Gun Company

Place	Date	Hour	Summary of Events and Information	Remarks and references to Appendices
In the Field	17/4		Later in the afternoon instructions were received that positions for direct fire covering the whole of our front were to be chosen. These were not to be on the front line but were chosen below in the open.	
	18th	5 am	Guns positions sited and work commenced at 8 p.m. No 3 Section inspected by Brigade Commander who in the ...	
	16th		Brigade Commander approved the sandparapet. Did not hole emplacement continued by night.	
	17th		Further positions sited for guns at the front line — M.G. emplacements to be constructed with the first two not being occupied.	
	18th		Under enton built No 1 Section entered and returned to Bn HQ Work carried on, ... emplacements by night.	
	19th		During the night Work of No 9 and 9end rendered difficult by heavy frost & what had been Yorks Ground trips hard Sandbags frozen.	
	20th		carried out by Section in reserve. ditto.	
	21st		ditto. Detachment of J. 199 Machine Gun Coy attached for instruction.	

A/OC 146th Machine Gun Coy

Army Form C. 2118.

WAR DIARY
or
INTELLIGENCE SUMMARY

146th Machine Gun Company

(Erase heading not required.)

Place	Date	Hour	Summary of Events and Information	Remarks and references to Appendices
			Baker Section relief to A Section returned to H.Q. and C. and could not get number further. The other parties with reinforcements returned as though with difficulty finished and	
	23rd		Work on then a fresh machine gun firing out in front. Work commenced at night that of targets received	
	24th		To night firing. Bank of Infantrymen carried out with difficulty owing to bad ground. Usual night firing trades carried out.	
	25th		Visit the Co. by Capt 6 Commander firing on RANSART in keeping guns from firing. In spite of usual machine gun opposition to the purpose & covering HQ barrel cross appears for an Barrel.	
	26th		Yellow section relief. No 4 Section returned to by HQ Registration & shipped trades carried out and completed for despatches to ADGT	
	27th		Nothing to report. Two other wants wounded by other fire.	
	28th		Enemy have been working with great activity in front of RANSART orders received to be on guard against a possible raid. Sections on the line warned & special precautions taken to keep guns company the suspected danger zone in action	
	29th		Nothing to report. Usual Light firing in enemy communications	

mw Lieut
mw 146 M.G. Coy

2449 Wt. W14957/Mgo 750,000 1/16 J.B.C. & A. Forms/C.2118/12.

Army Form C. 2118.

WAR DIARY
or
INTELLIGENCE SUMMARY

146th Machine Gun Company

(Erase heading not required.)

Place	Date	Hour	Summary of Events and Information	Remarks and references to Appendices
In the Field	Jan 30th		Orders received for two of boy transport to HUMBERCAMP. Arrangement made with Company on our right to accept in covering the portion of the front on which the enemy was masked of an intention to raid Turkish Section which No.3 section returned to H.Q.	
	31st	3.00	Arrangements made to move transport to HUMBERCAMP. Orders received for move to be carried out on 2nd February.	

31/1/17 -

Mitchell
Lieut
for O.C. 146 Machine Gun Coy.

Vol/14

SECRET.

WAR DIARY.

OF

146th Machine Gun Company

FOR

February 1917.

WAR DIARY
or
INTELLIGENCE SUMMARY

(Erase heading not required.)

11th Machine Gun Company

Place	Date	Hour	Summary of Events and Information	Remarks and references to Appendices
In the Field	Feb 16th 1917		Transport moved to HUMBERCAMP. Covered standings. One gun fired during night 1/2 hr from ROADWAR St on to gap in enemy wire from x y b 40. 60. to x y b 45. 90. Firing on enemy communications at night.	REF MAPS LENS 11 HAZEBROUCK 5A BLAIRVILLE 1/10,000
		2 am	Heavy guns down during cold weather. Suggestion that stove for heating guns forwarded to Division.	
		3 pm	Night firing on RANSART & enemy communications.	
		4 pm	Tommy Cookers sent up to front line guns. 1st Section relieved 4th Section.	RANSART, Loop Railway & MAISON 3/BUSTER
		5 pm	1 Section night firing that if a Tommy Cooker was held under the gun for 5 minutes in every 25 minutes the water in the barrel casing would not freeze. Of course, the rate the barrel casing depends upon the intensity of the cold. It was also found necessary to heat under the barrel that the barrel occasionally can however must be taken, that the burner is not placed under the extractor, as the minimum pressure by contraction forms a film of ice between the extractor & lock casing and prevents	
		6 pm	Left Batt. Adjut. stated it was suggested by Batt Adjut that the firing at night of guns close by, drew the shelling on RANSART & enemy communication lines. It is thought that the machine gun was first the cause of this shelling light firing on RANSART & enemy communication lines.	

WAR DIARY or INTELLIGENCE SUMMARY

Army Form C. 2118.

(Erase heading not required.)

Instructions regarding War Diaries and Intelligence Summaries are contained in F. S. Regs., Part II. and the Staff Manual respectively. Title Pages will be prepared in manuscript.

Place	Date 1917	Hour	Summary of Events and Information	Remarks and references to Appendices
In the Field	Feb 7th		Nothing to report. Lights firing on usual targets and on gaps in wire.	WORK
	8th		do	WORK
	9th		do	WORK
	10th		It may be well to remark here that the oil lubricating G.S. is very bad. It evaporates very quickly, leaving a residue which clogs the mechanism. Nothing to report. Lights firing on usual targets.	WORK
	11th		Attempts made by 1/5 Bn West York Regt. were too high. Identification was obtained. Consequently no C.M.G.O. of XVIII Corps visited line. Section relief to report. Lights firing on usual targets.	WORK
	12th			WORK
	13th			WORK
	14th			WORK
	15th		Nothing to report. Lights firing on usual targets.	WORK
	16th		do	WORK
	17th		Raids by 147th & 148th Brigades, no assistance given by this unit	WORK
	18th		Nothing to report. Lights firing on usual targets.	WORK
	19th		198th M.G. Coy arrived to relieve 146th M.G. Coy. Lights firing on RAMPART & WORK	WORK
	20th		Relief by 198th M.G. Coy commenced at 12 noon. Completed by 4.30 pm with the exception of one emplacement in Opera line.	

WAR DIARY
or
INTELLIGENCE SUMMARY

Army Form C. 2118.

Place	Date 1917	Hour	Summary of Events and Information	Remarks and references to Appendices
In the field	21st		emplacement was relieved at 6.30 p.m. One officer and one sergeant corporals and two men for gun team, were left in the trenches.	Roster
Le Souich	22nd		All Officers and men remaining in trenches reached Bdy. H.Q. at BAILLEULMONT at 10 a.m. Company marched to LE SOUICH. Good billets.	Roster Roster
do	23rd		Cleaning guns ammunition etc. General cleaning up.	Roster
do	24th		Inspection by G.O.C. 146th Infy. Brigade. The expressed his satisfaction.	Roster
Bouquemaison	25th		Moved to BOUQUEMAISON.	Roster
Croisette	26th		Moved to CROISETTE.	Roster
Bailleul-lez-Pernes	27th		Moved to BAILLEUL-LEZ-PERNES. Very good billets. Billeted in good barns and in a chateau.	Roster
Paquet-le-Grand	28th		Moved to PAQUET LE GRAND. C.O. and 4 section officers proceeded to LAVENTIE and viewed line to be taken over.	Roster

Austhball
Capt
Commdg 146 Machine Gun
Coy

Vol. 15

SECRET.

W. R. DIARY.

OF

146 Machine Gun Company

FOR

March 1917.

Army Form C. 2118.

WAR DIARY
or
INTELLIGENCE SUMMARY
(Erase heading not required.)

No. 146 MACHINE GUN COMPANY.

Instructions regarding War Diaries and Intelligence Summaries are contained in F. S. Regs., Part II. and the Staff Manual respectively. Title Pages will be prepared in manuscript.

Place	Date 1917 March	Hour	Summary of Events and Information	Remarks and references to Appendices
LE GRAND PACAUT	1st		The Company moved from Biéches to LAVENTIE. Nos 2, 3, & 4 Sections relieved 10 guns of the 169 Machine Gun Company on the FAUQUISSART Sector. Relief completed by 4 pm. Coy Headquarters established at LAVENTIE. There was no scheme of machine gun defence in the line.	REF. MAPS HAZEBROUCK 5A 1/100,000 AUBERS 36 S.W. 1 1/10,000
LAVENTIE	2nd		Nothing unusual.	FISRB FISRB
	3rd		Enemy machine guns were troublesome during the day. It was therefore decided to retaliate by firing a long burst whenever the enemy machine guns fired. Usual night firing.	FISRB
	4th		do	FISRB
	5th		do	FISRB
	6th		do	FISRB
	7th		Nothing to report. Usual night firing.	FISRB
	8th		The retaliatory fire by our guns during the day successfully stopped practically all enemy M.G. day firing. Usual night firing.	FISRB
	9th		Inter Section relief. 2 Sections came into reserve	FISRB
	10th		Nothing to report. Usual night firing.	FISRB
	11th		The sites and emplacements on the Corps line were inspected by G.S.O.1, 49th Div.	FISRB
	12th		Nothing to report. Usual night firing. A large amount of work has been done by the Army on the "WICK	FISRB

WAR DIARY or INTELLIGENCE SUMMARY

Army Form C. 2118.

No. 146 MACHINE GUN COMPANY.

Place	Date 1917	Hour	Summary of Events and Information	Remarks and references to Appendices
	March			
	12th		SALIENT. The right line of guns at M.18.d.99.18. were altered so as to cover the fosses and fences in position at M.18.d.10.50. Another gun was sent up	AWSR8
	13th		Nothing to report. Usual night firing.	AWSR8
	14th		do	AWSR8
	15th		Nothing to report. Usual night firing. Inter-section relief.	AWSR8
	16th		do	AWSR8
	17th		do	AWSR8
	18th		do	AWSR8
	19th		do Inter-section relief.	AWSR8
	20th		During the last three day's there has been much hostile trench mortaring in the Left Batt sector. This activity indicates possibly a raid. Usual night firing	AWSR8
	21st		Nothing to report. Usual night firing	AWSR8
	22nd		do	AWSR8
	23rd		No 3 Section relieved No 1. Night firing	AWSR8
	24th		Nothing to report. Usual night firing	AWSR8
	25th		do	AWSR8
	26th		All front line guns moved to selected positions in vicinity of B Lm Escombrible trench mortar activity	AWSR8

Army Form C. 2118.

WAR DIARY
or
INTELLIGENCE SUMMARY

(Erase heading not required.)

No. 146 MACHINE GUN "COMPANY."

No..........
Date..........

Instructions regarding War Diaries and Intelligence Summaries are contained in F. S. Regs., Part II. and the Staff Manual respectively. Title Pages will be prepared in manuscript.

Place	Date 1917	Hour	Summary of Events and Information	Remarks and references to Appendices
	MARCH		Enemy raid on our trenches at 11.15 pm. Driven off leaving 4 dead, from which valuable identifications were obtained. Enemy took to pinworms.	AISRB
	26th		New emplacements commenced. Night firing	AISRB
	27th		Two Portuguese officers + 1 N.C.O attached for instruction. Night firing	AISRB
	28th		Nothing to report. Night firing	AISRB
	29th		do.	AISRB
	30th		do.	AISRB
	31st		do. No 2 Sect. relieved No 4	AISRB

Aspinall
Capt.
Commanding 146th Machine Gun Coy.

SECRET.

WAR DIARY.

OF

146th Mach Gun Coy

FOR

April 1917.

Vol 16

Army Form C. 2118.

WAR DIARY
or
INTELLIGENCE SUMMARY
(Erase heading not required.)

1/16 L Manchester Fus Battn

Place	Date 1917	Hour	Summary of Events and Information	Remarks and references to Appendices
LAVENTIE	April 1st		Nothing to report. Night firing	REFMAP. AUBER 36SW 1/10,000
	2nd		do	
	3rd		do	
	4th		Enemy artillery extremely active all day, especially in front of right section J. Usual night firing	
	5th		Three Portuguese officers attached for instruction	
	6th		Enemy artillery very active in early morning on support line of Right Sector. Usual night firing	
	7th		Nothing to report. Usual night firing	
	8th		Usual night firing	
	9th		Portuguese officers returned to units. Usual night firing	
	10th		Nothing to report. Usual night firing	
	11th		do	
	12th		do	
	13th		do	
	14th		Night firing curtailed on a/c of condition of barrels & about	
	15th		suffery. Nothing to report. About 1000 ras. night firing	

Army Form C. 2118.

WAR DIARY
or
INTELLIGENCE SUMMARY
(Erase heading not required.)

46th Machine Gun Company

Place	Date	Hour	Summary of Events and Information	Remarks and references to Appendices
LAVENTIE	April 1916 16th		Nothing to report. About 1000 rds night firing	
	17th		do	
	18th		Few bombs supplied. night firing increased to 6000 rds	
	19th		Cpl Ball showed. Clonal night firing	
	20th		Nothing to report. Clonal night firing	
	21st		do do	
	22nd		do do	
	23rd		do do	
	24th		do do	
	25th		do do	
	26th		do do	
	27th		do do	
	28th		Major A.W. Bolton arrived to take over. Clonal night firing	
	29th		Nothing to report. Clonal night firing	
	30th		Lt G.W.D. Belgrave arrived. do (as summary officer)	

Alex Anderson Lieut.
O.C. 46th Machine Gun Company

for O.C. 46th Machine Gun Company

Army Form C. 2118.

Vol 17
146th Machine Gun Bat

WAR DIARY
or
INTELLIGENCE SUMMARY
(Erase heading not required.)

Instructions regarding War Diaries and Intelligence Summaries are contained in F.S. Regs., Part II. and the Staff Manual respectively. Title Pages will be prepared in manuscript.

Place	Date 1917	Hour	Summary of Events and Information	Remarks and references to Appendices
In the Field	May 1st		Conference Section Officers at Centre Section H.Q. re proposed raid on German trenches. Noting to report. Usual light firing.	
	2nd		Conference between C.O. and C.O.s of 199 & 148 M.G. Coys re proposed raid. Enemy raid on Right Sector, enemy did not obtain identification. One prisoner left in our hands. Usual light firing.	
	3rd		Inter-section relief. Your positions selected in own and Right Brigade area for cooperation during proposed raid. Usual light firing on enemy tracks, tramways etc.	
	4th		Nothing to report. Usual light firing.	
	5th		Positions for 8 guns in Right Bde. Sector Lewis gun fire laid by Lieut Bolsle and 2 Lt Oliver. Usual light firing.	
	6th		8 guns test by 148th M.G. Coy relieved 8 Lewis guns & Coy guns withdrawn from positions Nos 4, 7, 8, 10. Sec. C.O.B. 30 3/5/17 attached Lt Anderson proceeded on leave to England.	
	7th		C.O. Lt. Thompson & Pte Sams D.L. remaining at duty. C.O. went round both emplacements with the Brigade Commander to inspect sites for dug-outs.	

Army Form C. 2118.

WAR DIARY
or
INTELLIGENCE SUMMARY
(Erase heading not required.)

Instructions regarding War Diaries and Intelligence Summaries are contained in F. S. Regs., Part II. and the Staff Manual respectively. Title Pages will be prepared in manuscript.

Place	Date 1917	Hour	Summary of Events and Information	Remarks and references to Appendices
In the Field	May 7th		Raid carried out by 1/8th Bn. W.Y. Regt. the day co-operated (see attached O.O. 31) Raid successful, identification obtained, at least two Germans killed. Prisoner was a Pole. Lewis gun fired 50,250 rounds S.A.A.	
	8th		Three sections moved into the line in relief of the two sections of the 148th M.G. Coy. (See O.O. 32 attached)	
	9th		Nothing to report. Usual night firing.	
	10th		– do –	
	11th		– do – Each M gun quicker. 500 rounds at enemy	
			Usual night firing, 6000 rounds. Aircraft went indirect fire emplacement confirmed.	
	12th		Usual night firing, 4,500 rounds on roads and tracks in N 20 c & d, N 15 c & d & N 14 b.	
	13th		Usual night firing, 5000 rounds on targets in N 20 a & N 15 a & b.	
	14th		Usual night firing, 5000 rounds on cross roads in N 25 b, tramway and tracks in N 15 c & N 14 b & tracks in N 20 a.	
	15th		Usual night firing, 5,500 rounds on tracks & tracks N 15 c & N 14 d and cross roads in N 25 b, N 20 b, tramway & tracks in	
	16th		Usual night firing 6200 rounds on trenches and tracks in N 20 b, cross Roads at N 25 b, tramway and tracks in N 15 c & d & N 21 b.	

WAR DIARY
or
INTELLIGENCE SUMMARY
(Erase heading not required.)

Army Form C. 2118.

Place	Date 1917	Hour	Summary of Events and Information	Remarks and references to Appendices
In the Field	May 17th		Usual night firing. 4500 rounds on trenches in N20b, tramway & tracks in N15c, tracks in N21b & N15d, Cross Roads in N25b.	
	18th		Usual night firing 4000 rounds on trenches and cross roads in N20b and cross roads in N25b.	
	19th		Usual night firing 4500 rounds on trenches & tracks in N20a, tramway in N14d & N14c, cross roads in N25b. Two gun teams off to assist a raid by 1/5 Bn W.Yorks Regt.	
	20th		A raid by 1/5th Bn W.Y. Regt very successful. 6 prisoners taken 3 killed & no losses on our side. If one gun cooperated by firing on C.T. BERTHA, the road being used at the rear of the C.T. Usual night firing, on tramway and tracks in N14d & N15c, tracks in N20a & cross roads in N25b.	✗
	21st		✗ Prisoners state our Machine Gun fire is very accurate and that they received warning to keep 200 yds to the side of the roads when shelled by M. Guns. Bde Operation Order No 50 recd. The Coy is to be relieved tomorrow (22nd) by 199 M.G.Coy. 199 M.G. Coy. moved to ROBECQ at 1pm to take 4 Section (Lieut. Lynch) moved to ROBECQ in relief of a section of 199 Coy.	

Army Form C. 2118.

WAR DIARY
or
INTELLIGENCE SUMMARY

(Erase heading not required.)

Instructions regarding War Diaries and Intelligence Summaries are contained in F. S. Regs., Part II. and the Staff Manual respectively. Title Pages will be prepared in manuscript.

Place	Date	Hour	Summary of Events and Information	Remarks and references to Appendices
In the Field	May 1917 21st		Section of 199 M.G Coy arrived at 3.30 pm. Usual fight from 54000 rounds on trenches and tracks in N14d (This drew retaliation from enemy gun in direction of Sousa's House tracks in N20a & b and roads in N25b	
	22nd		Company relieved in the line by 199 M.G. Coy Relieving company marched to MERVILLE to confirmed by 2pm to 2 Section marched to MERVILLE to take up anti-aircraft duties. No 1 & 3 Section + H.Q. moved into rest billets at LEOBES. Lieut Anderson returned from leave.	
	23rd		Section Training, inspections etc.	
	24th		do	
	25th		do	
	26th		do	
	27th		do	
	28th		do	
	29th		do	
	30th		do	
	31st		do	

R.W. Bolton Major,
Commanding 146th Machine Gun Coy

SECRET.   Copy No. 2

146th MACHINE GUN COMPANY.

Reference Operation Order No. 30 dated 5/5/17.
_____

The relief will take place on 6/5/17.

The orders contained in the above Operation Order will hold good.

Also, orders given personally by the Commanding Officer to Section Officers on the morning of the 4th inst will be carried out.

H.W. Bolton Major

Officer Commanding 146th Machine Gun Coy

5/5/17.

Issued at

Copies to.
No. 1 to C.O.
    2   No. 1 Section.
    3   No. 2 Section
    4   No. 3 Section
    5   No. 4 Section.
    6   Transport Officer
    7   C.Q.M.S.
    8.   War Diary.
    9   Retained.
   10.   Ditto.

SECRET.   Copy No. 5.

                              146th Machine Gun Company.

Operation Order No. 60.   Ref Map AUBERS 36. S.W.1.
                    LEFT SECTOR.
───

1.   Gun teams at Nos. 1, 2, and 3 positions will be relieved by the
        148th Machine Gun Company on 4/5/17.

2.   Guides from these positions will be at the RED HOUSE at 10.0 a.m.

3.   When relieved these teams will carry guns and all equipment
        minus belt boxes to JOCK'S LODGE.

4.   Gun team at JOCK'S LODGE will not be relieved but will withdraw
        at 11.0.am.

5.   On conclusion of relieve and removal of Section stores No 3 Section
        will return to Coy. H.Qs. leaving all guns and equipment at JOCK'S
        LODGE.

6.   Usual handing over certificates and receipts will be
        obtained and forwarded to Coy H.Qs.

7.   Remainder of day's rations will be brought out.

8.   Relief will be reported to Coy H.Qs (146th Machine Gun Company)
        as soon as possible.

9.   O.C. No. 3 Section will arrange to receive guns of No. 1 Section at
        JOCK'S LODGE in accordance with Operation Order attached, and
        will arrange with incoming Officer for a suitable place for these to
        be kept.

10.   O.C. No. 3 Section will detail a Man to remain at JOCK'S LODGE to
        look after Section Stores. He will also detail 1 N.C.O. to be
        responsible for stores of No. 1 and 3 Sections.

11.   Acknowledge.

Issued at 10.0am.

   Copies to
   No. 1 to C.O.
      2 2 i/c Anderson.
      3 No. 3 Section
      4 War Diary.
      5.

3/5/17.

                                                        Lieut.
                                    for O.C. 146th Machine Gun Company.

SECRET.   Copy No. 5

                    240th Machine Gun Company.

Operating Order No. 30.   B.C.Hqs. 29.9.18. C.E.F.
==

                    NIGHT RELIEF.   No. V. Section.

1.   Gun Teams at positions Nos. 8,11 and 12 will be relieved by
     the 240th Machine Gun Company on 4/9/18.

2.   Gun team at No.10 position will not be relieved but will
     withdraw to Section H.Qs. at 11.0p.m. preparatory to returning
     with remainder of Section to Coy H.Qs.

3.   A guide from each gun team specified in para 1 will be at the GUN
     HOUSE at 20.0.p.m.

4.   On completion of relief, Section will return to Coy.H.Qs.

5.   All equipment except belt boxes will be brought out in all cases.

6.   The usual handing over certificates and receipts will be obtained
     and forwarded to Coy H.Qs.

7.   Limber transportation will be at THIEPVAL at 21.30 p.m. to
     transport guns etc to Coy HQ.

8.   Remainder of day's rations will be brought out.

9.   Relief will be reported to 15592 M.G.Coys Coy H.Qs. as soon as
     possible.

10. Acknowledge.

     Issued at 10.0 p.m.

                                              W.Mc Anderson
     Copies to
                                                    Lieut.
     No. 1   to O.C.   for O.C. 240th Machine Gun Company.
         2   Transport Officer
         3   No. V Section
         4   War diary.
         5.
         6.   Lt. Anderson.

SECRET.   149th Machine Gun Company.   Copy No.

Operation Order No. 20.   Ref Map AUBERS 20, S, W.

_____

1. The gun teams at Nos 3 and 5 positions will be relieved by the 149th
   Machine Gun Company on 4/5/17.

2. Guides from these positions will be at the RED HOUSE at 12.30.a.m.

3. On completion of relief these gun teams will carry guns and all
   equipment except belt boxes to JOCK'S LODGE and hand these over to
   2/Lt. JARVIS.

4. Gun teams at Nos 7 and 8 positions will not be relieved but will
   withdraw at 11.30.p.m. and guns and all equipment minus belt boxes
   to JOCK'S LODGE and hand these over to 2/Lt. JARVIS.

5. Lt. JUDE will detail 2 Men to remain at JOCK'S LODGE in charge of
   Section stores and will arrange for rations for remainder of day to
   be left for these men.

6. On completion of relief and removal of Section stores No.3 Section
   less 2 men specified in para 5 will return to Coy H.Q.'s.

7. The usual handing over certificates and receipts will be obtained
   and handed in to Coy O.C.
   Remainder of day's rations will be brought out.

8. ██

9. Relief will be reported to Coy H.Qs 149th M.G.Coy, as soon as
   possible.

10. Ack. Acknowledge.

    Issued at 12.0.a.m.
                                            W.Mc Andrew

Copies No.
   No.1 to O.C.
       Lt. Pattinson.
       No.2 Section.   for.O.C. 149th Machine Gun Coy.
       No.3 Section.
       War Diary.
    5.

    /E/Tb.

Copy No 9

SECRET.   7/5/17.

146th Machine Gun Company.
....

Special Operation Order. No.31.

Map Ref.: AUBERS.: 36. S. W. 1.

1. The 1/8th Bn. West Yorks Regt will carry out a raid against the enemy trenches on the night of 7/8th inst.

Time. 2. Zero hour will be 9-40p.m.

Cooperation
M. Gs. 3. At Zero barrages will be opened as follows:—

    8 Guns, under Lieuts' Bone & Oliver.
        M 24d. 70.20. to N 19c. 40.05.

    6 Guns, under Lieuts' Jarvie & Twynam.
        N 19c. 40.80. to N 19c. 30.14.

    2 Guns, under Lieut. King.
        N 19a. 32.18. to N 19c. 40.80.

Rate of 4. From Zero to Zero plus 10 300 rounds per min. all guns.
Fire.
    Zero plus 10 to Cease Fire. 200 rounds per min. 50% guns.

Cease Fire. 5. When Artillery Cease Fire.   (About Zero plus 20)

Return to 6. At Cease Fire the Right Party will return with all equipment
H. Q.   to Head Quarters.

    At Cease Fire plus 40 the Left Parties will return with all equipment to Head Quarters.

Synchroni- 7. A watch which has been set to correct time by O. C. Left Group
-zation.   R. F. A. will be sent to O. C. Raid, Trench Mortar Battery, Machine Gun Company, and Batt. H. Q. during the afternoon.

    Issued at 4.10 p.m.

Copies to :—
  No1. C. O.
    2. 146th Inf. Bde.
    3. 2/Lieut. Jarvie.
    4. 2/Lieut. Twynam.
    5. 2/Lieut. Oliver.
    6. Lieut. King.
    7. War Diary.
    8. Lieut. Bone.
    9. Retained.

                                                     Capt,
        For O. C. 146th Machine Gun Company.

146th Machine Gun Company.

7/5/17m

RELIEF TABLE.

Section.	Sector being relieved	Relieving gun positions. Nos.	Taking over gun position.	Rendezvous.	Remarks.
No 4 Section.	LEFT.	1, 2, 3.	4.	JOCKS LODGE.	
No 1 Section.	CENTRE.	5, & 6.	7, 8.	Junction of DEAD END ROAD and BACQUEROT RD.	
No 2 Section.	RIGHT.	9, 11, 12.	10.	Junction of RUE MASSELOT & BACQUEROT ROAD.	

S E C R E T.   Copy No. 9

                                                         7/5/17.

                    140th Machine Gun Company.
           ....

Operation Order No 32.   Ref. Map AUBERS 36. S.W.1.

---

1. Three Sections of the 140th Machine Gun Company will move into the line and relieve 2 Sections of the 148th Machine Gun Company on 8/5/17. (Relief Table attached).

2. Sections to be at rendezvous (see attached relief table) at 1-30p.m. No guides will be necessary.

3. The usual handing over certificates and receipts will be obtained and sent to Coy H. Q. as soon as possible.

4. The Transport Officer will make arrangements for limbers.

5. Completion of relief will be notified to Head Quarters by Code word "BONUS".

6. On relief 2 Sections of the 148th Machine Gun Company will return to H. Qs. 140th Machine Gun Company.

7. Acknowledge.

        Issued at..........p.m.

Copies to:-

    No 1. No 1 Section.
     2.   2   "
     3.   4.   "
     4. 2/Lieut. Thomas.
     5. 2/Lieut. Shinner.
     6. Transport Officer.
     7. C. Q. M. S.
     8. File.
     9. No 3 Section (for information).
    10. C. O.
    11. O. C. 148th. M. G. Coy.
    12. War Diary.
    13. Retained.

                                    AWBolton Capt.
                    For O. C. 140th Machine Gun Company.

Vol 18

SECRET.

WAR DIARY.

OF

146th Machine Gun. Coy.

FOR

June. 1917.

Army Form C. 2118.

WAR DIARY
or
INTELLIGENCE SUMMARY
(Erase heading not required.)

146th Machine Gun Company

Place	Date 1917	Hour	Summary of Events and Information	Remarks and references to Appendices
ZELOBES	June 1st	9 xx	Section Training.	REF MAP AUBERS 36 S.W.1. EDITION.8A
	3rd		"	
			Bde O.O. recd the Coy is to relieve 199th M.G. Coy in the line on the 4th inst. Tho 4 Section at ROBECQ moves to LAVENTIE today	
LAVENTIE	4th		Company relieved 199 M.G. Coy in the line see OO.38 attached. Our guns fired indirect during the night 5000 rounds upon N15c.1.8 to N16a.8.5 the vicinity of N20c.4.4 & Rue Delaval. N20a.9s.ys. 250 rounds were fired at a hostile aeroplane between 4 and 5 am causing it to retire.	
	5th		Usual night firing. 4450 rounds on BUTT HOUSE; N15c 65.33. to N15c.8s.65 & vicinity of N20b.15.60.	
	6th		Usual night firing. Between points of O.o.38 fired 5000 rounds on RUE DANTE N20b to N20d. IRMA TRENCH and TRACK N15c. 35.13. to N15c.6s.30 and CLARA TRENCH N19d. 25.60 to N19d 8.1.	
	7th		Raid by 1/4 Bn W.Y. Rot. 3 Officers 81 Other Ranks 11.15 p.m. In connection with raid 4 guns fired 10,050 rounds. See Programme O.O. attached	
	8th		Usual night firing 4000 rounds on H.Q. and TRACKS in N20d. RUE DANTE N 20.b. 35.05 to N.20.d.yo.6s. & TRACKS in N15c	

Army Form C. 2118.

WAR DIARY or INTELLIGENCE SUMMARY

(Erase heading not required.)

46th Machine Gun Company

Place	Date 1917	Hour	Summary of Events and Information	Remarks and references to Appendices
LAVENTIE	8th			
	9th		250 rounds also fired at hostile aircraft at 10.15 am. Usual night firing 4000 rounds on cross roads in N15c. tracks in N15c. + from N20b.2.5. to N20b.4.2	
	10th		C.O. accompanied A.M.G.O. round both lines & emplacements Usual night firing - 5000 rounds on Road & Track from N20 c B.S. to N26a 95.90. Tracks from N20 b 94.30 to N21a 08.6 S. and from N20 d 0.4. to N20 d 55.55.	
	11th		Cooperated with Brigade on our Right during raid. See programme attached 1900 rounds were fired	
	12th		Usual night firing 5000 rounds on N20b 94.30 to N21a 08.45; ROAD + TRACK IN N20c B.S. to N20a 95.90. N30b.42.60 N30b.28.S. BERTHA C.T. N20a.9y to N20b.30 DORA C.T. N25a 55.9S. to N26a 95.50 The tracks which are out of our own Bde SECTOR were fired on owing to RIGHT BDE sending up S.O.S. Signal.	
	13th		No 1 M.G. Coy. P.E.F. 3 OFFS + 36 N.C.O.s and men sent into the line Para 9 P.E.F attached for instruction Usual night firing 4 5000 rounds on N15c 2.1 to N21a6.S. N20 d 05.40. + N25b 25.55 to N25d 42.94.	
	14th		1 Section 199 (Div) MG. Coy reported they will be attached	

Army Form C. 2118.

WAR DIARY
or
INTELLIGENCE SUMMARY
(Erase heading not required.)

Instructions regarding War Diaries and Intelligence Summaries are contained in F. S. Regs., Part II. and the Staff Manual respectively. Title Pages will be prepared in manuscript.

Place	Date	Hour	Summary of Events and Information	Remarks and references to Appendices
LAVENTIE	14th		During a "shoot" usual night firing 4450 rounds on N20a9y to N20b3Oj. Enemy trucks in N15c25.08 to N15c95.50 and on Rue Delevel from Butt House to N20 c.b.5. Look over 6 aph emplacements	
	15th		12 x000 rcd. ords. O.O. 53 cancelled. The section 199 MG Coy returned to billets. In conjunction with Stokes Mortars 8,450 rounds were fired on enemy posts during the night. N20a69.89 to N20b 10.43. N19d 43.40. to N25b 86.96 N4C 40.12 to N20a9y N15c.5.5 to N15c 8.1	
	16th		Gun party of No 1 Portuguese MG Coy sent into the line for instruction. 1st party returned. Usual night firing 4500 rounds on CLARA C.T. from N.19.d. 43.40. to N25b 86.96. N 20 b 36.10 to N 20 d 45.30 and N15c 5.5 to N15c 8.1	
	17th		Usual night firing 5450. rounds upon ROAD JUNCTION at N20a35 N20a 95.96. IRMA'S ELEPHANT & ROAD BEND N14b. 950 rounds were fired at enemy aeroplanes	
	18th		Night firing. 4450 rounds on N20a9y N19a.5.1 & N.19c.14.85 & IRMA'S ELEPHANT & ROAD BEND in N14b. Also 1000 rounds upon enemy aeroplanes at 12-15 p.m. 4-30 am & 4-50 am	

Army Form C. 2118.

WAR DIARY
or
INTELLIGENCE SUMMARY

(Erase heading not required.)

Instructions regarding War Diaries and Intelligence Summaries are contained in F. S. Regs., Part II. and the Staff Manual respectively. Title Pages will be prepared in manuscript.

Place	Date	Hour	Summary of Events and Information	Remarks and references to Appendices
LAVENTIE	19th		Night firing — 9250 rounds upon tracks and trenches N14 c to N20 a. IRMA'S ELEPHANT & ROAD BEND in N14, tracks in N15c, CLARA'S FAN. CLARA CT. DORA TRENCH at N19c6.	
	20th		Night firing — 5,500 rounds upon tracks in N15 c to N21 a. CLARA'S FAN and CLARA CT. DORA TRENCH & N14 to N20 b. Also 150 rounds were fired at an enemy aeroplane at 4500 ft. Range 3000 ft. In connection with a raid on our right by the 148th Inf Bde special night firing targets were given. 12,000 rounds were fired on N20 b. 9.8 to N26 b.1. Y, N20 b.3.1 to N20 d.5.8. N14 a.8.8 to N15 c.4.0. N15 c.4.5 to N15 c.8.0. and CLARA TRENCH and DOTT HOUSE. The raid about 20 including one officer) prisoners were killed, and 3 unwounded prisoners who gave valuable information were taken. Unfortunately on their return happened an accident while coming across "No Man's Land". 100 rounds were fired upon an Army 'plane flying at 2500 ft — no result.	
	21st		A demonstration was given by No.1 Section at the XI Corps School on the Method of Photographing guns etc and ammunition on limbers, kit, animals and men. The Junior Course has now in this	

WAR DIARY or INTELLIGENCE SUMMARY

Army Form C. 2118.

Place	Date	Hour	Summary of Events and Information	Remarks and references to Appendices
LAVENTIE	22nd		Night firing:- 8,160 rounds were fired on DORB O.T. CLARA O.T. BUTT HOUSE, the railway & LONG BARN in N.15c. & N20a9y to N20b40. Both of this section's planes of our balloons were seen to be destroyed by enemy aircraft. The observers descended in parachute. In connection with the training of the Portuguese machine gunners attached to 1 Section returned the demonstration in methods of transport & tacks. N20a.y.6. to N20d.8.2, N21a.6.5. & ROAD BEND at N25b.5.5. 1000 rounds were fired at enemy aeroplanes at 5.50/m 6.0/m & 6.30/m.	
	23rd		An Erebut balloon was seen to be brought down in flames north of this sector by enemy aeroplane at 11.50 am. Graf hielt ALBRECHT reported for duty. Light firing:- 4,500 rounds were fired on IRMA'S ELEPHANT ROAD BEND from N.14b.4.1. to N.14b.7.0. Cross Roads at N20a.9.y & Road Junction at N20c.3.5.	
	24th		Three emplacements on the support line were occupied this morning by teams composed solely of Portuguese. Guns in the sector. 15 machine guns, Portuguese machine gunners this sector.	

Army Form C. 2118.

WAR DIARY
or
INTELLIGENCE SUMMARY

(Erase heading not required.)

Instructions regarding War Diaries and Intelligence Summaries are contained in F. S. Regs., Part II. and the Staff Manual respectively. Title Pages will be prepared in manuscript.

Place	Date 1917	Hour	Summary of Events and Information	Remarks and references to Appendices
LAVENTIE	25th		Posts were established at 2.30 am this morning in the enemy front line, at two points (Sugar Loaf and Wick Salient). Two more emplacements were occupied this morning by Portuguese bombing parties. 14 Stokes runs in the line and this sector h.d. fired 4,500 rounds were fired upon IRMA'S, ELEPHANT, + ROSEBEND in N14bN20c.3.5. to N20c.y.1. + N20 a.9.6. An enemy plane was driven back by 100 m.g. while flying at 2000 ft.	
	26th		No.24647 Pte Spivills H. (Stanner) accidentally killed No.26598 Pte Siddle R. (1st West Yorks) attd. M.G. Coy.) accidentally wounded. Right forearm:— An enemy m.g. was suppressed, special firing or combination reached H.Q.s etc., took place. 10,250 Rounds were fired on RUE DELEVAL in N14d back from N15c.2.1. to N 21 a. 9 y + RUE DANTE 150 m.g. were fired at and drove back an enemy plane flying at 2,000 ft.	
	27th		Night firing:— 5,000 rds were fired on tracks from N15c.20.10. to N 21 a.6.5. N25c35.60. MOSSY TRENCH from N14c 35.85 to RUE DELEVAL. 500 rounds were fired at enemy plane at 2500 ft. The plane was flying low and was driven right back	

Army Form C. 2118.

WAR DIARY
or
INTELLIGENCE SUMMARY

(Erase heading not required.)

Instructions regarding War Diaries and Intelligence Summaries are contained in F. S. Regs., Part II. and the Staff Manual respectively. Title Pages will be prepared in manuscript.

Place	Date 1914	Hour	Summary of Events and Information	Remarks and references to Appendices
LAVENTIE	28th		LT. WHITE proceeded to School of Military Engineering, CHATHAM. MAJOR BOLTON proceeded to CAMBERS to attend demonstration in M.G. Barrage fire. LIEUT ANDERSON took command during his absence. Night firing:- 3,500 rds were fired on trenches from N.146.b.6. to N.14.9.5. & from N.19.a.3.5. to N.19.d.8.1. 1250 rds were fired at enemy flare at 5 pm + 5.30 pm. Flare drawn back.	
	29th		Enemy used searching fire with 5.9 H.V. shells from M.5a.60.13 to M.4b.95.80. from 6 pm to 8.40 pm. Shells fell at intervals of about 3 minutes. A long Zouinger which was fired for some days was apparently the target. Night firing:- 4,500 rds on Rd Junction N.20.c.30.50, N.15c.70.35 to N.15c.86.05. & Roe Dante.	
	30th		Nothing to report.	

John Anderson
Lieut.
Commanding 146th Machine Gun Coy.

SECRET.   Copy No. 10.
                          146th Machine Gun Company.
                          ****

Operation Order No. 38.   Map Refs.   AUBERS, 36. S. W. 1.
                                                 FRANCE, Sheet 36. A.
_____

1.   The 146th M. G. Coy will relieve the 199th M. G. Coy in the line on
     the 4th June. 1917. ROBECQ
2.   No 4 Section at ~~MERVILLE~~ will be relieved by the reserve section of
     the 199th M. G. Coy on the 3rd June 1917. When they will proceed to
     billets in LAVENTIE.
3.   On arrival at LAVENTIE No 4 Section will come under orders of O. C.
     199th M. G. Coy and will relieve ~~one~~ section of that Coy in the line
     early on 4th June 1917.   LEFT
                         MERVILLE
4.   No 2 Section at ~~ROBECQ~~ will be relieved on the 4th June by one section
     of the 199th M. G. Coy, when they will proceed to billets in LAVENTIE.

5.   H. Q. and Nos 1 & 3 Sections will relieve two sections of the 199th
     M. G. Coy in the line on the 4th June 1917, parading as under:—
         No 1 Sec. Parade dress fighting order 6-45a.m. Packs will be carried
                      on limbers. (Arrives LAVENTIE Coy H. Q. at 8-30a.m.)
         No 3 Sec. Parade dress fighting order 7-15a.m. Packs will be carried
                      on limbers. (Arrives LAVENTIE Coy H. Q. at 9- 0a.m.)
         H. Q. Sec. Parade dress fighting order 7-45a.m. Packs will be carried
                      on H. Q. limbers. (Arrives LAVENTIE Coy H. Q. at 9-30a.m.)

6.   Guides for gun positions will be at Section H. Qs in each case.

7.   Transport.   Each Section will utilize its 3 Limbers in each case for
     transport of section stores to destinations.

8.   14 full belt boxes will be taken to each gun position.
     Ammunition.   S. A. A. will be taken over from the 199th Coy.

9.   Section stores which will not be taken into the line will be left in
     the fighting limbers, which will be parked at H. Q. LAVENTIE. S.A.A.
     limbers will return to transport lines, and will be parked there.

10. Rations for the 4th inst. will be carried under Section arrangements.

11. The following will be packed by 9-0a.m. on the 4th inst in the Q. M. S
     Stores ready for transport by motor lorry:-
         Q. M. Stores.   Orderly Room Stores.   Cobblers kit.
         Armourers Stores. Transport Stores not required on march.
         Canteen stores.   Officers valises.
     The following will accompany the motor lorry in charge of the above
     stores.
         S/Sgt. Partridge. Pte. Needes. Pte. Bishop.

12. Positions of Sections in the line.
         No 1 Section will take over RIGHT SECTOR.
         No 4 Section   "   "   " LEFT SECTOR.
         No 3 Section   "   "   " CENTRE SECTOR.
         No 2 Section will be in reserve.

13. "Relief complete" of sections in the line will be reported to Coy. H.Q.
     LAVENTIE by telephone, using code word "JUNE".

                                                              - 1 -

Operation Order No 38. (continued).

ACKNOWLEDGE.

Issued at......p.m.

Copies to:-

    No 1.   No 1 Section.
    No 2.   No 2   "
    No 3.   No 3   "
    No 4.   No 4   "
    No 5.   O. C.
    No 6.   146th Inf. Bde.
    No 7.   O. C. Div. Reserve.
    No 8.   O. C. 198th M. G. Coy.
    No 9.   War Diary.
    No10.   Retained.
    No 11.   "

(signed) Lieut
for Major,

Commanding 146th Machine Gun Company.

Number of Guns	Gun Position.	1st Target.	Time.	2nd Target.	Time	Remarks
1	N.2a.13.56.	CLARA C.T. From N19b.00.20. to N19d.25.60.	Zero. Minus 16 to Zero Plus Y	Junction of Clara C.T. and Rue Deleval. 100ˣ each way.	Zero Plus Y to cease fire.	
1	N.18a.32.50	CLARA C.T. From N19d.28.60 to N19d.88.00	Zero Minus 15 to Cease Fire.			
1	N.Y.a.25.05.	Area - Bosche Support N.19a.64.64. - Y.8.88. CLARA. C.T. From N.19a.64.64 to N.19a.82.46. From N19a 82.46. to N19b.00.40. Along Track to N19a. Y6.88	Zero to Zero Plus Y.	Rue Deleval. in N20c.	Zero Plus Y.	
1	N.Y.b.25.44.	— do —	Zero to Zero Plus Y	Rue Deleval in N20d. and junction of Rue Deleval	Zero Plus Y to cease fire.	Approved by Lt Col Jeffrey

S E C R E T

1. The following programme will be carried out in conjunction with a raid by 148th Inf. Bde. on our right, on the night of the 11/12th inst.

2. Zero hour will be notified later.

3. LEFT SECTION will fire on:-

   IRMA TRENCH from N14d. 85. 80. to N15c. 45. 08.

   CLARAS FAN. N19b.

   CENTRE SECTION will fire on:-

   BERTHA from N.14.c.45.10 to RUE DELEVAL.

   DORA from N.25.a.47.97. to N.25.a.88.60.

   MOSSY from N.14.c.8.4. to RUE DELAVAL.

   RIGHT Section will fire on

   EVA TRENCH from M.30.b.72.60 to M.30.d.98.98.

   BUTT HOUSE N.25.b.

   Rate of fire, Zero to Zero plus 7, Rapid.
           Zero plus 7 to "Cease Fire", Steady Rate.

4. "Cease fire" will be Zero plus 37. Guns will then continue usual night firing except that EVA TRENCH will be kept under constant fire by RIGHT Section until dawn.

11/6/17.

Lieut.
For.O.C.146th Machine Gun Company.

Vol 19

SECRET.

WAR DIARY.

OF

116 Machine Gun Company

FOR

July 1917.

No. 146
MACHINE GUN
COMPANY

146th Machine Gun Company

WAR DIARY
or
INTELLIGENCE SUMMARY.
(Erase heading not required.)

Place	Date	Hour	Summary of Events and Information	Remarks and references to Appendices
LAVENTIE	July 12th 1917		Lieut. Anderson proceeded to Camiers to attend the M.G. Course at the school. Lieut Thrush took over the duties of second in command in his absence. Lieut Colquhoun became acting O.C. D Section. At 6.30pm an invention by Lt. A.E. Thrush was shown to G.O.C. Bde by Major Bolton - a safety device to limit the lower elevation of a machine gun and for attachment to the LONGFIELD MOUNTING.	
		2 xx	Nothing to report. 5,500 Rds on CLARA CT. & N 14 d 8.9.	
		3 am	At 1.am the enemy bombarded the front line of the Right Bde & the Right Battn front of our Bde with artillery and trench mortars, the Boche did not enter on our Bde front. Machine Gun teams in the line stood to till 3.30am At boy H.Q. the reserve section (D SECTION) stood to, and the teams for the section limbers arrived from the transport lines & ready to move off within half an hour of being warned. 3000 rds fired on BOTT HOUSE & SOUSA TRENCH junction of roads N21a60 sb during the night	

No. 146
MACHINE GUN
COMPANY. Army Form C. 2118.

No..................
Date................

WAR DIARY
or
INTELLIGENCE SUMMARY.
(Erase heading not required.)

Instructions regarding War Diaries and Intelligence Summaries are contained in F. S. Regs., Part II. and the Staff Manual respectively. Title pages will be prepared in manuscript.

Place	Date	Hour	Summary of Events and Information	Remarks and references to Appendices
LAVENTIE	4th		Indirect firing 4500 rds into RUE DELEVAL N14a 85.65 to N14a 50.20, N20a.	
"	5th		The P.E.F. on our right expected an enemy raid & so our right and centre guns were ready to switch on to enemy C.T. at S.O.S	
"	6th		Indirect fire – 6000 rds on Light Rly and tracks at N14b.96 68, N14d 85. 80 to N15c 40. 08 and the DISTILLERY	
"	7th		Indirect fire – 1500 rds fired on N14b 60 10, 1500 with DISTILLERY, 450 on the TREE CLUMP and 1000 on SOUSA	
"	8th		5000 rds fired on CROSS ROADS N20 a 95.76, and N15c 70.34, to N15c 84.04 and N19d 60 40 to N19 d. 80.11 OO.N°47) made out – and handing over lists sent to all Sections. Preparation continued for move on the 10th inst. Right firing 4,500 Rds on to BUTT HOUSE, SOUSA & N14 d 90.62 to N14d 50.20.	
"	9th		D and B Sections relieved in the line by the 10th M.G. Coy P.E.F. See O.O.47)	
"	10th		A Section relieved in the line see O.O.47) Coy moved to billets in ESTAIRES after relief. Leaving LAVENTIE 2.0pm, arrived ESTAIRES 3.0pm.	

No. 146
MACHINE GUN
COMPANY

WAR DIARY
or
INTELLIGENCE SUMMARY.
(Erase heading not required.)

Army Form C. 2118.

Place	Date	Hour	Summary of Events and Information	Remarks and references to Appendices
ESTAIRES	11th		Coy training and cleaning up stores etc.	
"	12th		Bath for the whole Company. Kit inspections, equipment cleaning, squad drill.	
LESTREM.	13th		The Coy entrained at LESTREM. Train moved off 7.8 am, arrived at LOON PLAGE	
LOON PLAGE			MARDICK Area at noon. Marched to GRAND SYNTHE FARM. The Coy marched past the Divisional General at LOON PLAGE Station. Company under Canvas	
MARDICK.	14th		Training for all sections. Gun drill. Packing limbers, and demonstration with	
do.			Guldon backs.	
do	15th		Training as for 14th.	
do	16th		Company marched to LEFFRINCKHOUCKE 5.0 am, arrived at destination 9.30 am. The Commanding Officer and Lt Smith & 2/Lt Twynam reconnoitred the line near NIEWPORT.	
LEFFRINKOURCKE	17th			
			The Company moved from LEFFRINKOURCKE at 1.30 pm. Arrived at OOST DUNKERQUE 7.0 pm. The whole Company in a field at the West End of village	
OOST DUNKERKE.	18th		Cleaning up. Transport provided for 146 T.M.B. to take guns up to the line.	
do	19th		Company training. Cleaning up etc. until 4.0 pm preparatory to proceeding to the line. Forty men attached to the Coy from the 146th Inf Bde = 10 men from each Battn.	

No. 146
MACHINE GUN
COMPANY Army Form C. 2118.

WAR DIARY
or
INTELLIGENCE SUMMARY.
(Erase heading not required.)

Instructions regarding War Diaries and Intelligence Summaries are contained in F. S. Regs., Part II. and the Staff Manual respectively. Title pages will be prepared in manuscript.

Place	Date	Hour	Summary of Events and Information	Remarks and references to Appendices
NIEUPORT.	19th		Three Sections proceeded to trenches at 8.0pm - 8.15pm and 8.30pm respectively. Coy. H.Qrs., remainder of Coy. Transport etc. left at OOST DUNKERQUE. Company relieved the 96th Company, Machine Gun Corps. in the St GEORGES Sector. ee OO 47 attached.	
do	20th		Relief complete at 1-30 a.m. Remainder of Coy in reserve and Transport Section left OOST DUNKERQUE for COXYDE. Artillery activity on both sides. Zeuche reconnoitering of the gun positions by the C.O. and 2 Thresh.	
"	21		Artillery activity on both sides. Enemy planes also very persistent in their efforts to cross our front. Indirect fire on MASSIF FARM at N 33 c 5.5. No of rounds 1000. 9500 rounds were also fired on enemy aeroplanes during the day. Conference held at Coy H.Q. (Farm at M 32 D. 3025.) in the afternoon by E.M.G.O. XVth Corps, D.M.G.O. and C.O. to discuss new scheme of defence.	MAP REF. NIEUPORT 12 S.W.
"	22		Enemy artillery not quite so active during day. 11-0pm Enemy put down heavy barrage on front line system and attempted to raid our trenches	

WAR DIARY
or
INTELLIGENCE SUMMARY.
(Erase heading not required.)

Army Form C. 2118.

No. 146 MACHINE GUN COMPANY.

Place	Date	Hour	Summary of Events and Information	Remarks and references to Appendices
NIEUPORT	22nd		at M22 b.9.3. The attempt failed. Enemy heavily shelled NIEUPORT with a new type of gas shell. Heavy casualties caused amongst reserve troops. One man of the Coy slightly gassed. Preparations carried on for the new scheme of defence. Total number of rounds fired on the S.O.S. lines during and after the enemy raid. 32700 rounds.	
	23rd		Heavy shelling by the enemy chiefly 15cm 21cm and 28cm calibre. Enemy attempted to enter our trenches at M22 b.2.2. Attempt frustrated by Artillery and Machine Gun barrage. Machinegun targets as follows:– 2500 rounds on Cross Roads at M23 b.95.95. – 2500 rounds on ROAD JUNCTION at M18.a.15.30. – 2500 rounds on ROAD JUNCTION. N27a.31. and 500 rounds were fired at enemy planes during the day.	
	24th		Heavy shelling by both sides – Orders received that no less than 9000 rounds were to fired by night firing. During the day 500 rounds were fired at enemy planes. Machine Gun targets during the night as follows. 2500 rounds on ROAD JUNCTION at M24 b.10.60 – 3000 rounds on CROSS ROADS at M 23 b. 95. 90. – 3000 rounds on CROSS ROADS at N 27 c 30. 90.	

No. 146
MACHINE GUN COMPANY.
No..........
Date..........

Army Form C. 2118.

WAR DIARY
or
INTELLIGENCE SUMMARY.
(Erase heading not required.)

Instructions regarding War Diaries and Intelligence Summaries are contained in F. S. Regs., Part II. and the Staff Manual respectively. Title pages will be prepared in manuscript.

Place	Date	Hour	Summary of Events and Information	Remarks and references to Appendices
NEWPORT.	25.		NEWPORT again very heavily shelled with 5"-9's and 8" shells. Approximately 2000 shells being sent into the town which is now in ruins. Enemy aircraft also very active. Machine Gun firing throughout the night as follows. – 8500 rounds upon CROSS ROADS M.18 c 3.1. – Road from N.27 a 3.9. to N.27 c. 22.20 and H.Qs and tracks at M.17 c 80.87. 250 rounds fired at enemy planes during day.	
	26		Promulgation of F.G.C.M. of No 71704 Pte SMITH G.W. found guilty on charge of MURDER of a French Girl at NOUVEAU MONDE (P. de CALAIS) on May 23.1917. Sentence death. – Commuted to 15 years penal servitude by G.-O.-C. in Chief July 15/17. Machine Guns fired 8500 rounds on targets as follows. CROSS ROADS. M.18 c 3.1. – MASSIF FARM at N.33 c and M. 17 c 8.5. Hostile artillery again very active.	
	27.		Lt ANDERSON reported back for duty from Machine Gun Course CAMIERS. Preparations made for M. G. Barrage for raid on enemy trenches. Raid cancelled. Machine Guns fired as follows 7500 rounds on GROOTE BAMBURGH FARM, the ROAD in N.27 c and the JUNCTION of RAVEN LANE and RAVEN TRENCH.	

No. 146
MACHINE GUN COMPANY.
No. ....
Date ....

WAR DIARY
or
INTELLIGENCE SUMMARY.
(Erase heading not required.)

Place	Date	Hour	Summary of Events and Information	Remarks and references to Appendices
NEWPORT.	28th		Enemy artillery again active. 11-0 pm. Our raiding party entered enemy trench at M.24.d.9.2. but had to withdraw without securing any identifications. Our party suffered casualties. Machine Guns fired in conjunction with the raid as follows:— 15000 rounds upon RAVEN LANE, RAT POST, BRIDGE LANE, and NIEUWENDAMME FORT. 24000 rounds were fired upon S.O.S. lines between 2·0 and 4·0 am. 750 rounds were fired on enemy planes during the day, at 10-4·45 pm and throughout the night, the enemy heavily shelled M31, M32c, and NIEUPORT with Phosgene Gas shells.	
-do-	29th		Hostile artillery active. Orders received for move to new area received 10·0 am 2·0 pm. Move cancelled. The L.G. fired as follows, 7500 rounds on M18c 70-29 M.23.6.95,95 and N.33.c.4.5 & N.33.c.80-44½, also 500 rounds upon enemy aeroplanes during the day.	
-do-	30.		Great activity by our artillery – barrages being frequently put down on enemy trenches. Notice received of O.C. Company Major H.W.BOLTON being appointed to D.M.G.O. 32nd Division. M.Gs fired as follows:—	

No. 146
MACHINE GUN
COMPANY. C. 2118.

WAR DIARY
or
INTELLIGENCE SUMMARY.
(Erase heading not required.)

146TH MACHINE GUN COMPANY

Instructions regarding War Diaries and Intelligence Summaries are contained in F. S. Regs., Part II. and the Staff Manual respectively. Title pages will be prepared in manuscript.

Place	Date	Hour	Summary of Events and Information	Remarks and references to Appendices
NIEUPORT	30		6250 rounds on S.O.S. lines during night. Practice barrage by own artillery. 8·0 p.m.	
do	31		Between 2·0 and 4·0 a.m. M.Gs fired 8000 rounds upon S.O.S. lines in response to S.O.S signal. Enemy artillery not so active. Preparations for M.G barrage in conjunction with infantry attack. Orders received for relief of Company by 96th M.G Company on 2/3rd August.	

A.E. Thresh Lieut
a/to 146 Machine Gun Company
In the Field.

SECRET.   140th Machine Gun Company.   Copy No.

Operation Order No. 47.

1   The 140th Machine Gun Company will relieve the 96th Machine Gun Company in the line on the night 19th/20th of July 1917.

2   Sections will parade with gun equipment and transport as under:-

      C Section   8-0p.m. and will be at H.Qs 96th M.G.Coy at 8-0.p.m.

      B Section and
   2 gun teams of D Section
                      8-15p.m.   do   do   do   do   do   at 9-15p.m.

      A Section and
   2 gun teams of D Section
                      8-30p.m.   do   do   do   do   do   at 9-30p.m.

3   Sections may leave surplus Stores at Company H.Qs.

4. Sections will leave at Coy H.Qs in the line all tripods and 2 belt boxes per gun. Remainder of the belt boxes will be taken to the gun position.

5. The Transport Officer will arrange transport as under:-

      C Section .... 2 limbers .... at 7-45p.m.

      B Section .... 3 limbers .... at 8p.m.

      A Section .... 3 limbers .... at 8-15p.m.

Copies to

No 1 to O.C.
   2   Lieut Thresh.
   3   O.C. 96th M.G.Coy.
   4   140th Inf.Bde.
   5   War Diary
   6   do.

                                                               Lieut.
                                          for O.C. 140th Machine Gun Company.

Vol 20

SECRET.

WAR DIARY.

OF

446 Machine Gun Coy

FOR

August 1914

Army Form C. 2118.
No. 145
MACHINE GUN COMPANY.

No. ....
Date ....

246th Machine Gun Company.

WAR DIARY
or
INTELLIGENCE SUMMARY.
(Erase heading not required.)

Instructions regarding War Diaries and Intelligence Summaries are contained in F. S. Regs., Part II. and the Staff Manual respectively. Title pages will be prepared in manuscript.

Place	Date 1917	Hour	Summary of Events and Information	Remarks and references to Appendices
NIEUPORT	Aug 1st		Major J W Bolton appointed D.M.G.O. 32nd Div.	REF MAP. NIEUPORT
			Lieut Anderson assumes command of the Company, Lieut A.E.	1:25,000
			Thresh becomes 2nd i/c command. Usual night firing	Edition 2A.
	2nd		Rev preparations made for relief by 96th M.G. Coy. Relief	
			cancelled 5.30 p.m.	
	3rd		Company relieved by 96th M.G. Coy. After relief Coy proceeded	
			to OOST DUINKERKE for the night.	
	4th		Coy proceeded from OOST DUINKERKE, 1.30 p.m. passing LEFFRINCKOUCKE	
			8.30 p.m. stopping for tea at Y.M.C.A. Hut for BRAY DUNES	
			Cleaned up equipment, guns.	
			APPOINTMENTS. Lieut ANDERSON. W.A. is appointed O.C. Unit on	
			from 1/8/17.	
			Lieut THRESH. A.E. is appointed 2nd i/c of the	
			'Coy from 1/8/17.	
	6th		Company Inspection by O.C. Section. Parade under Section	
			Officers.	

Army Form C. 2118.

No. 146
MACHINE GUN
COMPANY

WAR DIARY
or
INTELLIGENCE SUMMARY.
(Erase heading not required.)

Place	Date	Hour	Summary of Events and Information	Remarks and references to Appendices
LEFRINCKOUCKE	5/1		Section Training	
	6th		Company Inspection by C.O.	
	7th		Company Training	
	8th		—do—	
	9th		—do—	
	10th		10am Church Parade at TETEGHEM	
	11th		Company Inspection by C.O.	
	12th		Company Inspection	
	13th		Inspection & transport by OC Div Train 1/2 CE Div Train who considered the best transport in the Div.	
	14th		Company marched from LEFRINCKOUCKE to TETEGHEM	
TETEGHEM 15th			Usual Parades. In a report sent in to the B. Inspection by OC Div Train of transports of the Bde the Div General remarked that he was very pleased with the report on this	
	16th		Company's transport by O.C. Div Train	
	17th		—do—	
	18th		Section training. Barrage drill. Lecture by Div Gas Off.	

Army Form C. 2118.
No. 146
MACHINE GUN
COMPANY

WAR DIARY
or
INTELLIGENCE SUMMARY.
(Erase heading not required.)

Instructions regarding War Diaries and Intelligence Summaries are contained in F. S. Regs., Part II. and the Staff Manual respectively. Title pages will be prepared in manuscript.

Place	Date	Hour	Summary of Events and Information	Remarks and references to Appendices
	18th cont.		to the C.O.'s and Officers of the Company at 2.30 pm.	
	19th		Usual Company training	
	20th		ditto	
	21st		Section training	
	22nd		ditto. Transport inspected by Divisional General who said he was pleased with the turnout – Practice attack by 1/5th Bn WEST YORKS R with 4 guns of "A" Section on the Land Dunes	
	23rd		Section training	
	24th		Practice attack by the 1/4th Bn WEST YORKS R on Land Dunes, in which 4 guns of "C" Section co-operated.	
	25th		"B" Section with "A" Section and 2 guns of "D" Section took part in the practice attack by the 1/8th Bn WEST YORKS R	
	26th		Church Parade. – Section training in afternoon.	
	27th		"C" Section took part in practice attack by 1/5th Bn WEST YORKS R. Preparations for move from TETEGHEM to GHYVELDE.	

Army Form C. 2118.

WAR DIARY
or
INTELLIGENCE SUMMARY.
(Erase heading not required.)

No. 146
MACHINE GUN
COMPANY

Place	Date	Hour	Summary of Events and Information	Remarks and references to Appendices
GHYVELDE	28th		Company moved from TETEGHEM to GHYVELDE at 9-0am arriving at destination 11-0am. "D" Section took part in practice attack by the 1/4th Bn WEST YORKS R. At 7.15pm Fire broke out at the billet occupied by "A" "B" and "C" Sections resulting in 2 barns being burnt down destroying unmasked corn, practically the whole of the equipment, guns, and stores of "A" "B" and "C" Sections. The whole Company worked till midnight until the fire was got under. "A" Section under an officer was on duty all night.	
	29th		Making out lists of stores to replace those destroyed yesterday. Taking the evidence for the Brigade HQs. "A" Section under an officer on duty all day at the scene of the fire.	
	30th		Carrying on with Salvage work in connection with the fire. Section training — in afternoon.	
	31st		Orders received for move to Camp in GHYVELDE - move completed by 4-0pm. Company under canvas.	

W Andrews Capt
Commanding 146 Machine Gun Coy.

Sergt War Diary No 21
of
146 Machine Gun Coy
for
September 1917.

NO. 148
MACHINE GUN
COMPANY
Army Form C. 2118.

WAR DIARY
or
INTELLIGENCE SUMMARY.

(Erase heading not required.)

146 Machine Gun Company

Instructions regarding War Diaries and Intelligence Summaries are contained in F. S. Regs., Part II, and the Staff Manual respectively. Title pages will be prepared in manuscript.

Place	Date	Hour	Summary of Events and Information	Remarks and references to Appendices
GHYVELDE (NORD)	Sept 1st		Company and Section training	SHEET 12 Begin
	2		-ditto-	
	3		Court of Enquiry held on the fire which occurred on the 28/8/17	
	4		Company and Section training	
	5		-ditto-	
	6		-ditto-	
	7		-ditto-	
	8		-ditto-	
	9		-ditto-	
	10		Company moved to Reinforcement Camp GHYVELDE.	
	11		Company and Section training	
	12		-ditto-. Departure of 2/Lt TWYNAM to U.K.	
	13		-ditto- 2/Lt MATTHAMS reported for duty.	
	14		Company and Section training	
	15		Orders received for the Company to take over Corps Defence duties relieving the 147th Machine Gun Company. Company training as usual.	

WAR DIARY
or
INTELLIGENCE SUMMARY.
(Erase heading not required.)

No. 146 MACHINE GUN COMPANY
Army Form C. 2118.

Place	Date	Hour	Summary of Events and Information	Remarks and references to Appendices
	16		Preparations for move.	
	17		Move to COXYDE-BAINS relieving the 148th Machine Gun Coy. 12:30pm relief complete. 2.0pm 2/Lt Mills N killed by Shellfire.	
	18		nr NIEWPORT-BAINS. Right Sector at NIEWPORT BAINS heavily shelled - no casualties. All sectors employed on repairs to Coast defences.	
	19		Burial of 2/Lt Mills N in British Cemetery at COXYDE.	
	20		Orders received for Company relief by 203 M.G. Company and Lewis gun teams of 2/9 MANCHESTER R and the 2/5 E. LANCS R.	
	21		Company relieved as above - Billets occupied for the night in COXYDE BAINS.	
	22		Move to LES MOERES. Move complete by 12:30pm.	
	23		Capt Anderson to CAMIERS to attend Barrage Fire demonstration. Normal Company training.	
	24		Company moved to TETEGHEM AREA - in accordance with 146 H Inf Bde Operation Order 71.	

No. 143
MACHINE GUN
Army Form C. 2118.

WAR DIARY
or
INTELLIGENCE SUMMARY.
(Erase heading not required.)

Instructions regarding War Diaries and Intelligence Summaries are contained in F. S. Regs., Part II. and the Staff Manual respectively. Title pages will be prepared in manuscript.

Place	Date	Hour	Summary of Events and Information	Remarks and references to Appendices
	25		Company move to WORMHOUDT.	
	26		Company move to NOORDPEENE.	
	27		Training and cleaning up. Capt Anderson rejoined Coy from Camiers.	
	28		Company move to TATEGHEM AREA being billeted in Val de ACQUIN.	
	29		Company training. Practice attack by 146 th Inf Bde - 16 guns employed.	
	30		Company move to to TATEGHEM village of to practice	

W Anderson
Capt
Commanding 146 M.G. Company

Vol 22

S E C R E T.

WAR DIARY.

OF

146th Machine Gun Coy.

FOR

1st to 31st October 1917

146 Infantry Brigade

> No. 146
> MACHINE GUN
> COMPANY.
> No. RS 560
> Date...........

Herewith War Diary of
this Company for the month
of October 1917.

W Alex Anderson
Captain
Commanding 146 Machine Gun Coy

31/10/17

No. 146
MACHINE GUN
COMPANY. C. 2118.

WAR DIARY
or
INTELLIGENCE SUMMARY.
(Erase heading not required.)

146 F Machine Gun Coy

Instructions regarding War Diaries and Intelligence Summaries are contained in F. S. Regs., Part II. and the Staff Manual respectively. Title pages will be prepared in manuscript.

Place	Date	Hour	Summary of Events and Information	Remarks and references to Appendices
In the Field	Oct 1st		The Company moved from TATEGHEM to ST MARIE CAPPEL. Billets in farm at U.18.d.5.4. (Sheet 27)	
	2		Company training &c	
	3		— Ditto —	
	4		— Ditto —	
	5		Company moved to WATOU (No 2 AREA) Road travel.	
	6		Company training &c	
	7		Preparations for the commencement of operations.	
	8		Company moved to VLAMERTINGHE. Transport to YORK CAMP near POPERINGHE	
	9		Company moved into line WEST of PASSCHENDAELE. 8 guns into barrage line and 8 guns to assembly positions preparatory to moving forward to the attack. A & B Sections with Lt THRESH, Lt KING and 2/Lt OLIVER in command went over the top. 5.20 am. Attack by 49th Division with 66th Division on the Right flank and HQ of Division on the Right flank [?]	

P. D. & L., London, E.C.
A.2330 Wt W80/M3672 30,000 4/17 Sch.53a Forms/C/2 18/14

No. 146
MACHINE GUN
Army COMPANY. 211B.

No..........
Date..........

WAR DIARY
or
INTELLIGENCE SUMMARY.
(Erase heading not required.)

Instructions regarding War Diaries and Intelligence Summaries are contained in F. S. Regs., Part II. and the Staff Manual respectively. Title pages will be prepared in manuscript.

Place	Date	Hour	Summary of Events and Information	Remarks and references to Appendices
	11"		No 1 Curain on LEFT flank. 1 objective reached on all front but M.G. fire held up the attack midway to 2nd Physical Casualties in the Coy 2 killed 13 wounded. Company relieved by the 2 New Zealand M.G Company. Back to billets in VALVERTINGHE.	
	12.		Company back to reserve in WINNEZEELE. (B. AREA)	
	13		Cleaning equipment. Horse ex.	
	14		Company Training ex	
	15.		Brigade inspection by 2nd ANZAC Corps Commander Lieut. Genl. Godley.	
	16		Company Training ex	
	17		-do-	
	18		Transport inspection by 146 Infantry Brigade Commander.	
	19		Company Training ex	
	20		-do-	
	21		-do-	

No. 146
MACHINE GUN
FORM COMPANY.

Army

WAR DIARY
or
INTELLIGENCE SUMMARY.
(Erase heading not required.)

Instructions regarding War Diaries and Intelligence Summaries are contained in F. S. Regs., Part II. and the Staff Manual respectively. Title pages will be prepared in manuscript.

Place	Date	Hour	Summary of Events and Information	Remarks and references to Appendices
	22		Company training etc	
	23		-do- -do-	
	24		-do- -do-	
	25		-do- -do-	
	26		-do- -do-	
	27		-do- -do-	
	28		-do- -do-	
			Move to STEENVOORDE (EAST AREA)	
	29		Company training etc	
	30		-do- -do-	
	31		-do- -do-	

In the field
31-10-17.

W. Alec Anderson
Captain
Commanding 146 Machine Gun Company

CONFIDENTIAL

No. 146
MACHINE GUN
COMPANY.

War Diary.

146th Machine Gun Company

November 1917

Confidential

Headquarters

146th Infantry Brigade.

> No. 146
> MACHINE GUN
> COMPANY.
> No. RS 798
> Date 30/11/17

    Herewith War Diary of this Unit for the month of November 1917

W. Alex Anderson

30/11/17
                         Captain.
             Commanding 146th Machine Gun Company

No. 146
MACHINE GUN
Army Form C. 2118.

WAR DIARY
or
INTELLIGENCE SUMMARY.
(Erase heading not required.)

4.6th Machine Gun [Company]

Place	Date	Hour	Summary of Events and Information	Remarks and references to Appendices
STEENVOORDE	1917 Nov 1st		Company Training etc.	
	2nd		do	
	3rd		do	
	4th		do	
	5th		do	
	6th		do	
	7th		do	
	8th		Company moved to SWAN AREA S.E. of Ypres.	
	9th		3 Sections to barrage positions - Transport, 1 Section & HQrs remaining at SWAN AREA	
	10th		Company relieved the 4th Australian M.G. Coy in front line on BROODSIENDE RIDGE. 2 casualties during relief. Nothing of importance to report. 3 wounded	
	11th			
	12th		Casualties - 2 killed, 3 wounded	
	13th		Nothing to report	
			do	

Army Form C. 2118.

WAR DIARY
or
INTELLIGENCE SUMMARY.
(Erase heading not required.)

Instructions regarding War Diaries and Intelligence Summaries are contained in F. S. Regs., Part II. and the Staff Manual respectively. Title pages will be prepared in manuscript.

Place	Date	Hour	Summary of Events and Information	Remarks and references to Appendices
	1917 Nov. 14th		Nothing to report. Casualties — 1 killed, 1 wounded	
	15th		do —	
	16th		do Casualties — 1 killed	
	17th		do —	
	18th		Moved to Barrage Positions	
	19th		Nothing to report. Usual line routine.	
	20th		do —	
	21st		do —	
	22nd		do —	
	23rd		do —	
	24th		do —	
	25th		do —	
	26th		Relief by 47th M.G. Company. Casualties 1 O.R. wounded	
	27th		Cleaning up etc. Overhauling guns, equipment etc.	
	28th		do —	
	29th		Company training	

Army Form C. 2118.

WAR DIARY
or
INTELLIGENCE SUMMARY.
(Erase heading not required.)

Instructions regarding War Diaries and Intelligence Summaries are contained in F. S. Regs., Part II. and the Staff Manual respectively. Title pages will be prepared in manuscript.

Place	Date	Hour	Summary of Events and Information	Remarks and references to Appendices
	1917 Nov 30		Company training	

A.W. Anderson
Capt.
Commanding 46th Machine Gun Company

WM 24

Secret

War Diary
of
146th Machine Gun Coy
From
Dec 1st 16 Dec 31st — 17

Army Form C. 2118.

MACHINE GUN COMPANY.

146 & Machine Gun Company

WAR DIARY
or
INTELLIGENCE SUMMARY.
(Erase heading not required.)

Place	Date	Hour	Summary of Events and Information	Remarks and references to Appendices
Chateau Belge	1917 Dec 1st		Cleaning guns, belts, stores etc	H23b.9.9 Sheet 28
	2nd		do	
	3rd		Preparations for move to trenches	
	4th		A & B Sections (8 guns) relieved 148th Lachine Gun Coy (8 guns) in fire	
			DECLEARE SECTOR	
	5th		Nothing to report. Usual line routine. Reserve Section employed on	
			reinforcing Camp Area	
	6th		do	
	7th		'C' Section (4 guns) relieved 4 guns 148th M.G. Coy in LONNAGST	
			LEFT SECTOR. Usual routine at reserve H.Q.	
	8th		Nothing to report. Usual routine.	
	9th		do	
	10th		do	
	11th		2 guns 'B' Section relieved by 2nd N.Z.M.G. Coy. Usual	
			routine at reserve H.Q.	
	12th		2 guns 'A' Section 4 guns 'B' Section relieved by 148th M.G. Coy	

No. 146
MACHINE GUN
COMPANY. Army Form C. 2118.

WAR DIARY
or
INTELLIGENCE SUMMARY.
(Erase heading not required.)

Instructions regarding War Diaries and Intelligence Summaries are contained in F. S. Regs., Part II. and the Staff Manual respectively. Title pages will be prepared in manuscript.

Place	Date 1917	Hour	Summary of Events and Information	Remarks and references to Appendices
	12th	8.45pm	Relief complete	
	13th		4 Guns "C" Section relieved by 147 M.G.Coy.	
	14th		Cleaning up guns, stores, etc. Throwing bomb in Canal Area.	
	15th		Usual training, cleaning etc.	
	16th		do	
	17th		do	Preparation for taking over Zonnebeke
	18th		Sector (12 guns)	
	19th		"B" & "D" Sections (12 guns) relieved 147th M.G.Coy (12 guns) in Zonnebeke Sector.	
	20th		Nothing to report. Usual line routine. Reserve section employed in improving Camp Area.	
	21st		do	
	22nd		do	
	23rd		"C" Section relieved "D" Section in line. "D" Section returned to Langhof Lines. Usual line routine.	
	24th		Usual line routine. Reserve section employed in improvements to	

Army Form C. 2118.

WAR DIARY
or
INTELLIGENCE SUMMARY.
(Erase heading not required.)

Instructions regarding War Diaries and Intelligence Summaries are contained in F. S. Regs., Part II. and the Staff Manual respectively. Title pages will be prepared in manuscript.

Place	Date	Hour	Summary of Events and Information	Remarks and references to Appendices
	1917 Dec.			
	24th		Cant area	
	25th		Nothing to report. Xmas dinners	
	26th		do	
	27th		do	
	28th		do	
	29th		do	
	30th		Coy (2 guns) relieved by 49th M.G. Coy. Relief complete	
	31st		3rd and 3rd cnc.	

Names & H. for Capt.
Commanding 4th Tractor Gun Coy.

Vol 25

146 M Gun Coy.
War Diary.

Army Form C. 2118.

WAR DIARY
or
INTELLIGENCE SUMMARY.

146th Machine Gun Company

(Erase heading not required.)

Place	Date 1918	Hour	Summary of Events and Information	Remarks and references to Appendices
BELGIAN CHATEAU (CANAL AREA)	Jan 1st		Nothing to report. Cleaning guns & stores. Fatigue parties employed on improving Camp Area	D23b99 Sheet 28
	2nd		do	
	3rd		do	
	4th		Preparation for relief of 147th M.G. Coy (8 guns) by 5th inob. C. & D. Sections (8 guns) relieving 8 guns 147th M.G. Coy	ZONNEBEKE
	5th		on line BECELAERE SECTOR. Relief complete 5.30 p.m.	Sheet 28 NE 1/10000
	6th		Nothing to report. Usual night firing & line routine. Reserve Sections employed on improving Camp Area	
	7th		do	
	8th		do	
	9th		"A" Section relieved "D" Section in front line positions. "D" Section relieved "C" Section in barrage positions. Usual night firing. "C" & "D" relief returned to Reserve at Belgian Chateau.	
	10th		Usual line routine & night firing. Reserve Sections	

Army Form C. 2118.

WAR DIARY
or
INTELLIGENCE SUMMARY.
(Erase heading not required.)

Instructions regarding War Diaries and Intelligence Summaries are contained in F. S. Regs., Part II, and the Staff Manual respectively. Title pages will be prepared in manuscript.

Place	Date	Hour	Summary of Events and Information	Remarks and references to Appendices
	9/8			
	10th		Employed on improving Camp Area.	
	11th		Double line created & Night firing. Casualties 1 Killed 1 OR Wounded	
	12th		Preparation for the relief of the Company by the 1st M.G. Coy.	
	13th		8 gun Lot 2 M.G. Coy. relieved "A"&"D" Section in line. Relief complete 6.30pm. "A"&"D" Section returned to rest billets at Belgian Chateau. Preparations for move of Coy to Reserve Area, STAPLE AREA.	
	14th		Transport Section left at 4 am. "D" Section marched "A","B"&"C" Sections moved by bus at 11 am. to KRAMERTINGHE RAILHEAD to entrain for HAZEBROUCK.	
HAZEBROUCK	15th		Company (less "D" Section) arrived HAZEBROUCK at 1pm. "D" Section arrived HAZEBROUCK at 1pm & marched billets Sheet 27 U18b 3.3	
	16th		at gym. Overhauling, checking & cleaning equipment & stores. Company Training. Sports.	
	17th		Kit Inspection. Company Kit & Stores.	
	18th		Company Training. Sports.	

Army Form C. 2118.

WAR DIARY
or
INTELLIGENCE SUMMARY.

(Erase heading not required.) 146" Machine Gun Company

Instructions regarding War Diaries and Intelligence Summaries are contained in F. S. Regs., Part II. and the Staff Manual respectively. Title pages will be prepared in manuscript.

Place	Date	Hour	Summary of Events and Information	Remarks and references to Appendices
	19th		Company training. Practice now by "D" Section complete with Transport & above.	
	20th		Company training. Sports	
	21st		do do	
	22nd		do do	
	23rd		"A" & "B" Section practice on range. "C" & "D" Sections usual training. Inspection of Transport by G.O.C. 49th W.R. Division. Turnout reported very good.	
	24th		Company training. Bath.	
	25th		do do	
	26th		Inspection of Company by C.O. Company training. "C" & "D" Section range practice.	
	27th		Church Parade. Sports.	
	28th		Company training. Sports.	
	29th		do do	
	30th		Baths. Company attended Flame Projector Demonstration.	

Army Form C. 2118.

WAR DIARY
or
INTELLIGENCE SUMMARY.   146th Machine Gun Company

(Erase heading not required.)

Instructions regarding War Diaries and Intelligence Summaries are contained in F. S. Regs., Part II, and the Staff Manual respectively. Title pages will be prepared in manuscript.

Place	Date	Hour	Summary of Events and Information	Remarks and references to Appendices
	30		Sports.	
	31st		Company training Sports.	

A.E. Thresh. Lieut.
Commanding 146th Machine Gun Company

War Diary
of
146 Mach Gun Coy
for
February 1918

CONFIDENTIAL.

WAR DIARY.

OF

146th MACHINE GUN COMPANY.

FROM - 1-2-18   TO - 28-2-18.

WAR DIARY
or
INTELLIGENCE SUMMARY.
(Erase heading not required.)

No. 140
MACHINE GUN
COMPANY. Army C. 2118.

Instructions regarding War Diaries and Intelligence Summaries are contained in F. S. Regs., Part II. and the Staff Manual respectively. Title pages will be prepared in manuscript.

Place	Date 1918	Hour	Summary of Events and Information	Remarks and references to Appendices
STAPLE AREA	Feb 1st		Company was billeted & transport details to move to Staple Area. Moved to Moulle Area entraining at Eblinghem at 4pm to take part in demonstration at Ranges	WD 2 3 Sheet 27
Moulle	2nd		Nothing to report. Training as usual in Moulle Area	
	3rd		do	
	4th		12 Guns & teams in trench attack with battalions in congs	
	5th		Company moved from Moulle Area at 9 a.m. and arrived in billets in Staple Area at 4pm	
	6th		Company training	
	7th		do — One Section took part in Brigade smoking tournament	
	8th		Company training	
	9th		Company inspected and usual training	
	10th		Church Parade	
	11th		Company training	

WAR DIARY or INTELLIGENCE SUMMARY.

No. 146 MACHINE GUN COMPANY Army Form C. 2118.

Place	Date	Hour	Summary of Events and Information	Remarks and references to Appendices
Staple	Feb 12th 1918		Company training	
Arneo	13"		do do	
	14"		do	
	15"		Rifle practice on Range	
	16"		do	
	17"		Company training	
	18"		do	
	19"		do	
	20"		Preparation for move to trenches	
	21"		Company less transport proceeded to Caestre by road. Coy of Staple at 1pm arriving at Caestre at 4.15pm Coy horse marched billets on Swan Area at 7.15p Transport through to Swan Area by 10a.m.	
	22"		A, B & D Sections (12 guns) relieved 8 guns 3rd N.Z.M.G. Coy & 4 guns 4th N.Z.M.G. Coy - A Sections front line, B D Section support positions.	

No. 146
MACHINE GUN
COMPANY.

Army Form C. 2118.

WAR DIARY
or
INTELLIGENCE SUMMARY.
(Erase heading not required.)

Place	Date	Hour	Summary of Events and Information	Remarks and references to Appendices
LONNE BERG SECTOR	1/16 22nd		Usual line routine. Casualties 30R. Relvd by Sher. Sive	
	23rd		Usual line routine	
	24th		"C" Section relieved "D" Section in fort line positions	
	25th		"D" Section returned to rest billets in SWAN AREA	
	26th		Usual line routine. Reserve Section employed in improving	
			Camp Area	
	27th		do	
	28th		do	

26/2/18

A E Threet Lieut.
O.C. 146th Machine Gun Company

www.ingramcontent.com/pod-product-compliance
Lightning Source LLC
Chambersburg PA
CBHW081425160426
43193CB00013B/2197